The Quaker Invasion of Massachusetts

Richard P. Hallowell

HERITAGE BOOKS
2007

HERITAGE BOOKS
AN IMPRINT OF HERITAGE BOOKS, INC.

Books, CDs, and more—Worldwide

For our listing of thousands of titles see our website
at
www.HeritageBooks.com

A Facsimile Reprint
Published 2007 by
HERITAGE BOOKS, INC.
Publishing Division
65 East Main Street
Westminster, Maryland 21157-5026

Copyright © 1883 Richard P. Hallowell

Originally published by
The Riverside Press, Cambridge:
Electrotyped and Printed by
H. O. Houghton and Company

— Publisher's Notice —
In reprints such as this, it is often not possible to remove blemishes from the original. We feel the contents of this book warrant its reissue despite these blemishes and hope you will agree and read it with pleasure.

International Standard Book Number: 978-1-55613-085-4

PREFATORY NOTE.

THE object of this little volume is to correct popular fallacies and to assign to the Quakers their true place in the early history of Massachusetts. Any one who consults it with the expectation of finding a detailed and harrowing recital of every case of suffering by the Friends will be disappointed. This branch of the subject is treated only so far as is necessary to illustrate the mode of persecution resorted to by the Colonial authorities and the spirit in which it was resisted by the Quakers.

In addition to Puritan laws and other documents already published by the State, the Appendix contains some very interesting evidence never before published, and much material which, while it may be familiar to students who have made the subject one of special inquiry, will be both new and instructive to the general reader.

R. P. H.

BOSTON, MASS., 4th mo., 1883.

CONTENTS.

CHAPTER I

INTRODUCTORY. — THE RISE OF QUAKERISM . . . . PAGE 1

CHAPTER II.

THE INVASION. — MEASURES OF RESISTANCE AND DEFENSE 32

CHAPTER III.

THE WARFARE 56

CHAPTER IV.

CHARACTER AND CONDUCT OF THE INVADERS. — MODERN REVIEWERS REVIEWED 69

CHAPTER V.

THE CAUSE OF THE WAR, AND ITS RESULTS 117

APPENDIX.

Colonial Laws for the Suppression of Quakers 133
Petition for Severer Laws against the Quakers, October, 1658 153
The Examination of Quakers at ye Court of Assistants in Boston, March 7, 1659-60 157

CONTENTS.

	PAGE
James Cudworth's Letter, written in the Tenth Month, 1658	162
The Story of Hored Gardner	172
Recapitulation of the Sufferings of Laurence and Cassandra Southick	173
A Brief Sketch of the Sufferings of Elizabeth Hooten	177
Order for sending Quakers out of the Jurisdiction; together with the Petition of John Rouse, John Copeland, Samuel Shattock and others to the King for interference	182
Abstract from Joint Letter of William Robinson and Marmaduke Stevenson	202
Letter of Mary Dyer	206
Abstract of Letter from William Leddra, written to his Friends on the Day before his Execution	208
Daniel Gould's Letter	210
Letter from Mary Traske and Margaret Smith, accusing the Government	213
John Burstow's Letter	217
Letter from Josiah Suthick, a Quaker, to the Deputies assembled in the General Court	220

THE QUAKER INVASION OF MASSACHUSETTS.

CHAPTER I.

INTRODUCTORY. — THE RISE OF QUAKERISM.

PURITANISM, as the word implies, originated in an effort to purify the Protestant Christian Church. It inaugurated a reform almost as radical as the Protestant Reformation.

At a later day the name was narrowed in its significance, and was applied only to those who adhered to Calvinistic doctrines of religion, and attempted to establish both in Old and New England a theocracy based upon the Mosaic law and other teachings of the Old Testament. It was the parent, however, from whose loins issued the brood of religious sects which, as we shall see, divided the English people into hostile camps, and ultimately bequeathed to us the religious liberty we now enjoy.

Under Queen Elizabeth, and notwithstanding her repressive measures, Puritanism secured a permanent foothold in the English nation, and before the death of James I. it had become a mighty power. The introduction of the Bible into every cottage in the land inaugurated a revolution of which the end is not yet. All other literature was subordinated to the Old and New Testaments. During the greater part of the seventeenth century the people abandoned themselves to the consideration of questions appertaining to civil and religious liberty, and to the solution of religious problems. Ecclesiasticism, intrenched in the government, disputed with bitterness and ferocity every step of the people in the direction of freedom. The daring but abortive effort of Laud to bring about a reconciliation between Rome and the Anglican Church contributed largely to the overthrow of Charles I., and ended in the execution of both the Archbishop and his master.[1] The bigotry and cruelty of Laud were matched by the bigotry and cruelty of the Presbyterian. Milton be-

---

[1] See account of Laud's trial. Neal's *History of the Puritans*, Toulmin's edition, vol. iii. p. 231.

queathed to us an epigram that will live until religious intolerance ceases to plague the world. It runs, " new Presbyter is but old Priest writ large."

During the period of the Commonwealth toleration was fostered by the genius of Sir Harry Vane, and in a measure by Oliver Cromwell, but during those years and the succeeding reigns of Charles II. and James II., coercion and persecution, as well as political intrigue, played a conspicuous part in the vain effort to stay the progress of free inquiry and to arrest the development of liberal principles. Dissent increased under the stimulus of restraint and persecution. The middle of the century was a period of intense excitement. The spirit of controversy seemed to possess all classes. Thousands of controversial books and tracts were published. Parliament turned aside from the consideration of state affairs to discuss questions of religion. The courts of justice were continually the arena of religious debate. Itinerant preachers addressed multitudes of eager men and women in public houses, in the market-place, in barns, and in the open fields. The churches were filled with congregations gathered not only to hear aggressive sermons delivered by regular pastors, but to listen to the harangues of speakers representing other sects. At Leicester, in 1648, no less than four different sects met in the parish church for the purpose of religious disputation. Officers of the Parliament army, after exhorting their soldiers in camp-meetings, visited the churches and there assumed the *rôle* of clergymen. One of the tenets of the Independents was that " any gifted brother, if he find himself qualified thereto, may instruct, exhort, and preach in the church," and laymen constantly had access to the pulpit. It was not uncommon for some one, after the usual service, to rise in his place and proceed with his own exposition of the law and the gospel. This was done by Episcopal divines as well as by non-conformists. It is on record that, in 1656, Dr. Gunning, afterwards Regius Professor of Divinity at Cambridge and Bishop of Ely, went into the congregation of John Biddle, " the father of English Unitarians," and began a dispute with him.[1]

George Fox was a frequent visitor at the " steeple-house." On very rare occasions he

---

[1] Supplement to Neal, vol. iii. p. 556.

imitated the example of the Bishop, but it was his custom to wait quietly until the minister had ended, when he would often be invited to speak. The sects grew and multiplied. The enumeration of them as classified by Masson [1] is well worth reproduction. Beside the Papist who was faithful to Rome and the Churchman who was loyal to the bishops, there were Presbyterians, Independents, Baptists or Anabaptists, Old Brownists, Antinomians, Familists, Millenaries or Chiliasts, Expecters and Seekers, Divorcers, Anti-Sabbatarians, Traskites, Soul-Sleepers or Mortalists, Arians, Socinians and other Anti-Trinitarians, Anti-Scripturists, Skeptics or Questionists, Atheists, Fifth Monarchy Men, Ranters, The Muggletonians, Boehmenists, and Quakers or Friends.

The ferment of religious and irreligious speculation was something prodigious. In 1645 one Thomas Edwards, a prominent Presbyterian, who is described as a "fluent, rancorous, indefatigable, inquisitorial, and, on the whole, nasty kind of Christian," published the "Gangræna," a catalogue one of hundred and seventy-six miscellaneous "er-

[1] *Life of Milton*, vol. iii. pp. 143-159; vol. v. pp. 15-28.

rors, heresies, and blasphemies " of the sectaries, and during the following ten years many others might have been added to the list.

Mysticism and materialism, devout piety and impious scoffing, noble conceptions and shallow theories of liberty, honest self-abnegation and Pecksniffian cant, all found utterance in the babel of voices that resounded through the nation. It was an age when, as Milton phrases it, men undertook " to reassume the ill-deputed care of their religion into their own hands again."

Inevitably, in such a transition period, fanaticism played a conspicuous part. It manifested itself in whipping, scourging, mutilation of the bodies of offenders, in long imprisonments, — some men and women living for years in noisome and filthy gaols, — and in the confiscation and destruction of property. Weak minds were unhinged by it, and men of strong intellects, and ordinarily of sober judgment, defended and even committed excesses, both in speech and action, that to us, when they do not seem supremely ridiculous, are simply incredible.

Robert Barclay, author of the well-known " Apology," an able " explanation and vindication" of Quakerism, was one of the few controversial writers of that period whose books are still read with interest and profit. He was the peer of the best scholars, an admirable logician, and subtle even to profundity. A contemporary describes him as a man "sound in judgment, strong in argument, cheerful in sufferings, of a pleasant disposition, yet solid, plain, and exemplary in conversation. He was a learned man, a good Christian, and able minister, a dutiful son, a loving husband, a tender and careful father, an easy master, and good, kind neighbor and friend."

It taxes our credulity to believe that such a man, even in such an age, could, in any serious degree, be possessed by the spirit of fanaticism, but even as late as 1672, being overpowered by a sense of what he conceived to be religious duty, he walked through the streets of Aberdeen covered with sack-cloth and ashes. We read with a feeling of pity akin to sympathy, his explanatory address to the people. "I was," he says, "commanded of the Lord God ... great was the agony of my spirit . . . I besought the Lord with tears, that this cup might pass away from me . . . and this was the end and tendency of my testimony, — to call you to repentance by this signal and singular step, which I, as to my own will and inclination, was as unwilling to be found in, as the worst and most wicked of you can be averse from receiving or laying it to heart." He further explains that he acted " after the manner of some of the ancient prophets, and with similar motives." It was accounted a great virtue by the Puritans to imitate the ancient prophets, and they searched their Bibles for names as well as for example and divine law.

Hebrew names were almost as familiar to the ears of that generation as the names of Patrick and Bridget are to our own. It was said that the genealogy of Jesus might be learned from the names in Cromwell's regiments, and that the muster-master used no other list than the first chapter of Matthew.[1]

In Brome's " Travels," a book published in the latter half of the seventeenth century, the author, with evident intent to ridicule these manifestations of pious enthusiasm, professes to have seen the following names on a jury list in Sussex: " Accepted Tre-

[1] Neal, vol. iv. p. 96.

vor, Redeemed Compton, Faint-not Hewit, Make-Peace Heaton, God-Reward Smart, Hope-for Bending, Earth Adams, Called Lower, Kill-Sin Pimple, Return Spelman, Be-Faithful Joiner, Fly-Debate Roberts, Fight-the-good-Fight-of-Faith White, More-Fruit Fowler, Stand-Fast-on-High Stringer, Graceful Herding, Weep-not Billing, and Meek Brewer." Neal, Hume, and other historians accept this list as one of genuine baptismal names. Forster, in his "Statesmen of England," recognizes its true character, but believes that Brome was the victim of a joke, and that he reports the names in good faith. It is more probable, however, that he was the perpetrator, not the victim of the jest, for after reciting the list, he says soberly, and as if to justify his humor, " I myself have known some persons in London and other parts of this kingdom who have been christianed by the names of Faith, Hope, Charity, Mercy, Grace, Obedience, Endure, and Rejoice," and he might have added, Praise-God, for such was the name of a member of Oliver Cromwell's Parliament.

Fanaticism revived old and enacted new laws under which churches and cathedrals were despoiled with ruthless barbarism : images, pictures, painted glass, organs, copes, and fonts were mutilated or destroyed. Frenzied and pious Puritans drove horses, swine, and calves into the churches and baptized them with mock solemnity. They tore up the surplice as a remnant of Babylon and burned the book of "Common Prayer."[1] In the Puritan "Anatomy of the Service-Booke" we read, "As they are altars of Baal, erected and maintained by Baalites or Balaamites, so they, and all their ceremoniall accoutrements, and the Service-Booke itself, are an abomination." The Litany is styled, "not the least sinful, but rather the most offensive" part of the Liturgy.[2]

Bible phraseology was incorporated into ordinary speech; tracts and treatises were full of it, orators adopted it, state papers and proclamations were embodied in it. Scriptural and unscriptural denunciation and invective were legitimate weapons of warfare, and the pens of controversialists were often dipped in gall. Not only ignorant and obscure writers, but men conspicu-

[1] Marsden's *Later Puritans*, pp. 55–57. Brome, p. 258. Coit's *Puritanism*, p. 61.
[2] Coit, pp. 51–59.

ous for their piety, learning, and refinement, used language bitter, harsh, extravagant, and offensive to good taste. The Rev. Dr. Daniel Featley, a Presbyterian and a member of the historic Assembly of Divines at Westminster, published a tract in 1644, entitled " The Dippers dipt; or the Anabaptists ducked and plunged over head and ears at a disputation in Southwark," in which he calls the Baptists an idle and sottish sect; a lying and blasphemous sect; an impure and carnal sect; a bloody and cruel sect; a profane and sacrilegious sect.[1] In the same year he petitioned the House of Lords that John Milton might be cut off as a pestilent Anabaptist.

Prynne ridiculed the church choir in set terms. He said, " Choristers bellow the tenor, as it were oxen; bark a counterpart, as it were a kennel of dogs; roar out a treble, as it were a sort of bulls; and grunt out a bass, as it were a number of hogs."[2]

Milton says of the bishops, " they . . . shall be thrown down eternally into the darkest and deepest gulf of hell . . . the trample and spurn of all the other damned

---

[1] Quoted in Ivimey's *Milton*, p. 104.
[2] Quoted in Coit's *Puritanism*, p. 455.

... shall exercise a raving and bestial tyranny over them ... they shall remain in that plight forever, the basest, the lowermost, the most dejected and down-trodden vassals of perdition." [1] In his reply to Salmasius, who, in 1649, published a vindication of Charles I., he calls him a "pimp" and a "starving rascal," and denounces him in quaint but vigorous verse thus: —

"And in Rome's praise employ his poisoned breath,
Who threatened once to stink the Pope to death." [2]

It would be both pleasant and profitable to pause a moment to contemplate Puritanism in its larger and nobler aspect, but it has a place in this treatise only so far as it relates to Quakerism. The preceding sketch of the religious enthusiasm and fanaticism that marked its rise and progress, it is hoped, will serve a twofold purpose. Though necessarily incomplete, it will aid us to a better understanding of the nature and significance of the conflict between the Founders of Massachusetts and the Quakers, when we come to consider it, and in the mean time it will, in a measure, indicate some of the conditions under which Quakerism was developed.

[1] Coit, p. 455.   [2] Ivimey, p. 146.

George Fox was the founder of the sect. Macaulay, utterly unable to understand or appreciate this remarkable man, can " see no reason for placing him, morally or intellectually, above Ludowick Muggleton or Joanna Southcote." He thinks his intellect was " too much disordered for liberty, and not sufficiently disordered for Bedlam." Carlyle, with a deeper insight, recognizes in Fox a religious genius and reformer. " This man, by trade a shoemaker," he says, " was one of those to whom, under ruder or purer form, the Divine Idea of the Universe is pleased to manifest itself, . . . who therefore are rightly accounted Prophets, God-possessed. . . . Let some living Angelo or Rosa, with seeing eye and understanding heart, picture George Fox on that morning when he spreads out his cutting-board for the last time, and cuts cowhides by unwonted patterns, and stitches them together into one continuous case, the farewell service of his awl! Stitch away, thou noble Fox ; every prick of that little instrument is pricking into the heart of slavery and World-worship, and the Mammon god. Thy elbows jerk, as in strong swimmer's strokes, and every stroke is bear-

ing thee across the Prison-ditch, within
which Vanity holds her Work-house and
Rag-fair, into lands of true Liberty; were
the work done, there is in broad Europe
one Free Man, and thou art he!" Fox's
parents were members of the Established
Church, and were noted for their probity
and piety. He was born in Leicestershire,
England, in 1624. His school education
was limited and insufficient. Very early
in life he manifested a serious disposition,
sometimes bordering upon melancholy. His
pious mother, instead of luring him on to
the enjoyment of childish sports, encouraged his precocity, and, as a consequence,
he was never a boy in anything but years.
The child was father of the man. He was
honest almost to a fault. He would not re-
sent an affront, but never flinched in times
of trial. "Verily," with him, stood for
protestation and determination, and it was
a common remark among his companions,
that, "if George says 'Verily,' there is no
altering him." At the age of nineteen, and
for three continuous years, he experienced
mental suffering that would have unseated
an intellect less vigorous and rugged. He
withdrew from all companionship, but was

soon made miserable by the reflection that he had forsaken his relations. Returning home, he spent much of his time in solitary meditation and prayer. The Bible was his favorite, and almost his only study. His condition, he tells us, was often one of absolute despair. He consulted preachers of the various denominations, but found them " miserable comforters." He likens them to " an empty, hollow cask." The outcome of this mental conflict was the conviction that the paramount object of human existence is to get into a proper spiritual relation with the Creator. The moral faculties are to be quickened, the law of Love must govern our relations with our fellow-men; but a spiritual oneness with the Deity attained, the rest would follow as naturally as light follows the rising sun. He learned that the divine law is written upon the hearts of men; and that to construe or interpret it correctly, he must give heed to the voice of God in his own soul. His mission was now revealed to him. "I was commissioned," he says, " to turn people to that Inward Light — even that Divine Spirit which would lead men to all truth."

This doctrine of the Inward Light was

the corner-stone upon which Fox builded and upon which Quakerism rests. It was no new doctrine. Neither Fox nor his associates laid claim to a discovery. It was older than Christianity itself, but since the days of Jesus and his followers, it had been a mere theory, subordinate to doctrines embodied in the creeds. Jesus, in substance, taught the same lesson, but the Christian Church had forgotten it. Christ had come to be God and the Bible, the only revealed word. Fox sought to restore primitive Christianity by calling upon men not to forsake Jesus, but to worship God and to realize, in full, the relation to Him implied when we call him Father. The epithet, heretic, has so often been applied to the early Quakers that it is frequently assumed that they formally denied and denounced theological opinions alleged to be fundamental. This is a serious error. It is true they were not creed bound. "Where the Spirit of the Lord is, there is liberty," and liberty of conscience, liberty to think and to speak, not only found protection in a Quaker meeting, but zealous advocates and defenders wherever a Quaker voice was heard. Such liberty inevitably develops variety of opinion, and there was more latitude among the Friends than within the narrower limits of other sects. They all, however, believed in Father, Son, and Holy Ghost; in Christ the Saviour; in the atonement; in the resurrection; and in the inspiration of the Bible. Nevertheless, they held that " the letter killeth, but the Spirit giveth life," and that to interpret the written word, men must be inspired by the Spirit that guided the hands of those who wrote it. Fox said "the holy men of God wrote the Scriptures as they were moved by the Holy Ghost; and all Christendom are on heaps about those Scriptures, because they are not led by the same Holy Ghost as those were that gave forth the Scriptures; which Holy Ghost they must come to in themselves and be led by, if they come into all the truth of them." Barclay, in his " Apology," declares, " We do firmly believe that there is no other gospel to be preached, but that which was delivered by the apostles. . . . We distinguish betwixt a revelation of a new gospel and new doctrines, and a new revelation of the good old gospel and doctrines; the last we plead for, but the first we utterly deny." He is careful, however, to maintain the supremacy of the Spirit, and in this connection he assures the reader that some of his friends, " who not only were ignorant of the Greek and Hebrew, but even some of them could not read their own vulgar language, who being pressed by their adversaries with some citations out of the English translation, and finding them to disagree with the manifestation of truth in their own hearts, have boldly affirmed the Spirit of God never said so, and that it was certainly wrong; for they did not believe that any of the holy prophets or apostles had ever written so; which, when I, on this account, seriously examined, I really found to be errors and corruptions of the translators; who (as in most translations) do not so much give us the genuine signification of the words, as strain them to express that which comes nearest to that opinion and notion they have of truth." On another page he says the Scriptures " may be esteemed a secondary rule, subordinate to the Spirit, from which they have all their excellency and certainty; for as by the inward testimony of the Spirit we do alone truly know them, so they testify that the Spirit is that Guide by which the saints are led into all truth; therefore, according to the Scriptures, the Spirit is the first and principal leader."

The famous Richard Baxter, in a discussion with some Quakers, referring to this Inward Light, asked them, "If all have it, why may not I have it?" And a learned Unitarian clergyman of Boston calls this " one of his most pertinent questions." If so, Baxter must have been sorely pressed and at his wit's end for argument, for the Quakers could not too strongly urge the universality of the Divine Spirit, and their response no doubt was, that having it, he should *heed* it. Heed it, friend Baxter, and it will lead thee into all truth. The difficulty lay in his denial of it.

The logic of this cardinal principle of Quakerism led straight to repudiation of the authority of an ordained ministry, to the withdrawal from church membership, and the refusal to pay church tithes. Intellectual training alone cannot fit men to be religious teachers. The Spirit of God must first illuminate their souls and sanctify their lives. The Puritans rebelled against prelacy, and held in special abhorrence the forms and ceremonies borrowed from Rome by the English Church. Coming into power, they established their own church and compelled an unwilling people to conform to and support it. The Quakers probed deeper. They rebelled against prelate and presbyter alike. They claimed not toleration, but liberty of conscience for all as an inalienable right; they demanded the absolute separation of Church and State; denounced the clergy as priests and hirelings, and in spite of fiendish persecution refused to acknowledge their authority or to contribute so much as a farthing to their maintenance. Where the Spirit of the Lord is, there is liberty; and the spirit of liberty was infectious. Others as well as the Quakers asserted the religious equality of men and the sufficiency of the Holy Spirit, and with stinging invective exposed the pretenses of pious charlatans. In 1658, John Milton, in an address to Parliament, said, "For now commonly he that desires to be a minister looks not at the work but at the wages . . . it were much better there were not one divine in the university, nor no school divinity known; the idle sophistry of monks, the canker of religion. . . . But most of all are they to be reviled and shunned who cry out with the distinct voice of hirelings, that if you settle not our maintenance by laws, farewell the gospel; than which nothing can be more ignominious, and, I may say, more blasphemous against our Saviour, who hath promised without this condition both his Holy Spirit and his own presence with his church to the world's end." He continues, " Of which hireling even, together with all the mischiefs, dissensions, troubles, wars, merely of their own kindling, Christendom might soon rid herself and be happy, if Christians would but know their own dignity, their liberty, their adoption, and let it not be wondered if I say their spiritual priesthood, whereby they have all equally access to any ministerial functions whenever called by their own abilities and the church, though they never came near commencement or university."

These bold, brave words might well have been uttered by Fox, or Burroughs, or Thomas Ellwood, the Quaker reader to the blind old poet.

With remarkable unanimity the early Quakers held many views of religious obligation that brought them into direct conflict with the civil authorities and social usages. These views were known as "testimonies," and later, when an organization was effected, they were incorporated into what is known as the Discipline of the Society. Church ordinances, baptism, communion table, prayer-book, were contemned. Silent meditation, interrupted only by a short prayer or exhortation by one or more of them, who, perchance, were moved by the Spirit, constituted their only form of worship. They substituted simple affirmation for the oath, defending the innovation with apt and telling quotations from Scripture. They held meetings for worship, and were generally careful to abstain from all unnecessary secular employment on the first day of the week, but they did not regard it as especially the "Lord's day." They claimed that "all days are alike holy in the sight of God." They regarded the use of the plural number in addressing one person as a species of flattery, and adopted the simple thee and thou of the Bible. Your Holiness, Your Grace, Your Honor, etc., were "flattering titles," and therefore they addressed all men by their Christian names only. They declared "that it is not lawful for Christians to kneel or prostrate themselves to any man, or to bow the body, or to uncover the head to men. That it is not lawful for a Christian to use superfluities in apparel, as are of no use, save for ornament and vanity. That it is not lawful to use games, sports, plays, nor, among other things, comedies, among Christians, under the notion of recreations, which do not agree with Christian silence, gravity, and sobriety." They considered war " an evil as opposite and contrary to the Spirit and doctrine of Christ as light to darkness," and they would not fight. They laid particular emphasis upon the sacredness of the married relation, nevertheless their bigoted persecutors denounced Quaker marriages as illegal until in 1661 the courts confirmed the legality of such marriages. Even as careful a writer as Masson says "they had no religious ceremony in sanction of marriage."[1] Professor Masson, as his context proves, had ample opportunity to avoid this blunder, and it can only be accounted for on the theory that his mind is prejudiced by the still popular notion that the presence and offices of an ordained minister are necessary to make a marriage ceremony religious and

[1] *Life of Milton*, vol. v. p. 25.

to secure the Divine sanction of the nuptial rites. The Quakers thought otherwise. They repudiated the claims of the clergy, and believed that God alone can join men and women in the solemn covenant. "It is their custom," says Sewel, "first having the consent of the parents or guardians . . . and after due inquiry, all things appearing clear, they in a public meeting solemnly take each other in marriage, with a promise of love and fidelity, and not to leave one another before death separates them. Of this a certificate is drawn, mentioning the names and distinctions of the persons thus joined, which, being first signed by themselves, those then that are present sign as witnesses."[1] This custom is still in force, and, with some unimportant verbal amendments, the phraseology of early Friends is still preserved. After an appropriate silence, the groom and bride rise, and taking each other by the hand, each in turn repeats, "In the presence of the Lord and this assembly, I take thee to be my wife (or husband), promising, with Divine assistance, to be unto thee a loving and faithful husband (or wife) until death shall separate

[1] *History of the Quakers,* vol. ii. p. 408.

us." For religious solemnity and tender, touching simplicity, the Quaker marriage ceremony has always challenged comparison, and if any one desires to *feel* and realize the presence of God in a public or private gathering, let him attend a Quaker wedding.

One of the most popular slanders current is the charge that the early Quakers held all civil authority in contempt and were willful law-breakers. So far from this, they were an eminently law-abiding people, and had profound respect for the office of the civil magistrate. For the insignia of office they had, perhaps, too little regard, but for law on which social order and well-being depend, they showed a most exemplary fidelity. George Fox said, " Magistracy is for the praise of them that do well. . . . Magistrates are for the punishment of evildoers. . . . We are not against, but stand for all good government." Edward Burroughs, in 1658, wrote to Richard Cromwell, " As for magistracy, it was ordained of God to be a dread and terror and limit to evil-doers, and to be a defense and praise to all that do well, to condemn the guilty and to justify the guiltless." In an interview with the

King, in 1660, Richard Hubberthorn said, " Thus do we own magistrates ; whatsoever is set up by God, whether king, as supreme, or any set in authority by him, who are for the punishment of evil-doers, and the praise of them that do well, such shall we submit unto and assist in righteous and civil things, both by body and estate, and if any magistrates do that which is unrighteous, we must declare against it, only submit under it by a patient suffering and not rebel against any by insurrections, plots, and contrivances." Barclay's statement of the attitude of the early Quakers toward the civil law and the magistracy is equally clear and definite. He said, " Since God hath assumed to himself the power and dominion of conscience, who alone can rightly instruct and govern it, therefore it is not lawful for any whosoever, by virtue of any authority or principality they bear in the government of this world, to free the consciences of others, . . . providing always, that no man, under the pretense of conscience, prejudice his neighbor in his life or estate, or do anything destructive to, or inconsistent with, human society ; in which case the law is for the transgressor, and justice is to be administered upon all without respect of persons." Perhaps it should be stated here that because Barclay was a highly educated gentleman, and wrote his best known works as late as 1673–76, some modern critics insinuate, if they do not broadly affirm, that he does not fairly represent the Quakerism of 1656 to 1662. Such criticism is flagrantly unjust. It is alleged that "the crude and indigested notions which the early Quakers uttered 'in a prophetical way,' sounded like the wildest rant, to be relieved of the reproach of blasphemy only by being referred to a besotted stupidity or a shade of distraction."[1] With a magician's power, Barclay, it seems, transformed distraction into sobriety. At his touch besotted stupidity was metamorphosed into a wise intelligence, and blasphemy into reverential religion. This magician, and also William Penn, we are informed, "wrought out for the Friends a religious system for belief and practice, which would do honor to any fellowship of Christians at the present time." The simple truth is, that calumnies almost as harsh as the one just quoted, marred the writings of distinguished

[1] *Massachusetts and its Early History*, p. 106.

divines in the seventeenth, as well as in the nineteenth century. Barclay, recognizing vital religious truth in the " principles and doctrines" contemptuously called " notions " by our critic, wrote, not only an "explanation," but a " vindication " of them. He was a warm personal friend and admirer of Fox, and was admirably fitted for the task by education, sympathy, suffering, experience, and knowledge. It would be a difficult task for any one to show wherein the " religious system for belief and practice," elaborated by him, differs in essential particulars from the Quakerism of Fox, or Burroughs, or Hubberthorn. There is a striking correspondence in their opinions concerning social duty and the limit of their obligation to civil government; and, bearing in mind the fact that they were not anchored to a creed, we cannot but be impressed by the harmony of their doctrinal views. But this is a digression. The reader who cares to pursue the matter further should consult Barclay's " Catechism," his "Anarchy of the Ranters," and his " Apology." And for Penn's testimony as to the " extraordinary understanding in divine things," and the " admirable fluency and taking way of expression," so characteristic of the "first Quakers," one should read his "Rise and Progress of the People called Quakers."

Having noted some of the more salient features of Quakerism, we are quite prepared to believe that in an age of intense religious excitement some of its more ardent professors were victims of religious zeal, and occasionally were guilty of acts inconsistent with proper decorum. It must be added, too, that, when pushed in argument, prominent Friends, including Fox and Penn, justified some of these acts by throwing responsibility for them upon the Spirit of the Lord. On the other hand, they disowned James Naylor and others on account of their fantastic extravagances.[1] The number of Quakers was counted by tens of thousands, and at one period forty-two hundred of them were in the gaols,[2] not for any crime or misdemeanor, but because of their stout defense of liberty and their heroic resistance to religious tyranny. When driven or dragged from their meeting-houses, they assembled in the streets; and when the

[1] Sewel's *History*, vol. i. p. 177.
[2] Janney's *Life of Fox*, p. 477, and many other Quaker histories.

meeting-houses were torn down they met on the ruins, from whence they were driven only by personal violence. Many of them died in prison and many more suffered long imprisonment only to resume their life of sacrifice and trial when released. They were courageous, aggressive, bold, and unsparing in their denunciation of sin and sinners, but equally tender-hearted, loving, and affectionate. Even women suffering the tortures of the lash could kneel and ask God to forgive the wretched men who dealt the blows.[1]

The name Quaker was applied to them in derision, but as indicative of their character and aim, they called themselves Friends. When they organized, it was not in order to proclaim a creed or to build up a sect, but for humane purposes, and, in Fox's phraseology, for the " promotion of purity and virtue." The only test of membership was an habitual attendance at religious meetings. If a stranger appeared in their business meetings and wished to participate therein, he was asked for a certificate from Friends of his own town, indorsing, not his soundness in doctrine, but his personal

[1] *New England Judged*, p. 61.

character. "This precaution," says Fox, "was to prevent any bad spirit that may scandalize honest men, from bringing reproach upon them."

Questions of policy were not settled by a count of noses or a show of hands, but, after grave deliberation and conference, by what appeared to be the weight or solid judgment of the assembly.

Quakerism in its social and moral aspect was the synonym for brotherly love, purity, simplicity, integrity, and benevolence. The early Quakers not only advocated an enlightened revision of the criminal laws and a reform in the treatment of prisoners, which was then barbarous, but they visited the prisons, and sought out and aided the poor, the friendless, and the outcasts of society. They literally loved both friend and foe. Hated, reviled, and persecuted of men, they asked a divine blessing for their bitterest enemies.

CHAPTER II.

THE INVASION. — MEASURES OF RESISTANCE AND DEFENSE.

It is believed that numbers of the people of the town of Salem, in Massachusetts (together with others of the Plymouth Colony), had embraced the tenets of the Quakers prior to the arrival of some missionaries in 1656, but there is apparently no evidence to indicate that they had proclaimed themselves or adopted the name of the despised sect. Had they done so, they probably would have been at least named in the recommendation of the Court made in May of the same year, that " the 11th day of June next . . . be kept as a public day of humiliation, to seek the face of God in behalf of our native country, in reference to the abounding of errors, especially those of the Ranters and Quakers," etc. This is the first reference to the Friends found in the printed official records. When it was made, Plymouth Colony had been settled thirty-five years, and the Massachusetts Bay Colony, a quarter of a century. Roger Williams, who, with all his shortcomings, is fairly ranked with the apostles of liberty, had been driven into exile. Mrs. Ann Hutchinson had been suppressed and banished. Sir Henry Vane had returned to England discouraged and disheartened. Coddington, one of the founders, and afterwards a Quaker, had taken refuge in Rhode Island, where he enjoyed the liberty of conscience denied him here. Winthrop had died lamenting the part he had played in persecuting heresy.[1] Sir Richard Saltonstall, another founder, had addressed his famous letter, from England, to his old friends, in which he deplored their "tyranny and persecution," and besought them "not to practise those courses in a wilderness which you went so far to prevent."[2] His advice, it is needless to say, was unheeded. John Endicott was Governor, and John Norton the leading minister

---

[1] George Bishop's *New England Judged*, p. 226. First published in 1661, reprinted in 1667, with addition of a Second Part. Again reprinted in 1702 and bound in one volume with John Whiting's *Answer to Cotton Mather*, etc. For references in this book, see the edition of 1702.

[2] *Hutchinson Papers*, pp. 401-407.

of the Massachusetts Colony, when the first two Quaker visitors arrived, and the policy of repression found in them the sternest of supporters. Ann Austin and Mary Fisher came here in a vessel, in July of 1656. The laws referring to Quakers had not yet been enacted, and there was no law, human or divine, to prohibit their coming here or bringing their books with them. On the contrary, the " Body of the Liberties," enacted in 1641, was a guaranty of ample protection by the authorities if they were disturbed or molested. The prefatory declaration reads: " We do therefore, this day, religiously and unanimously, decree and confirm these following rights, liberties, and privileges, concerning our churches and civil state, to be respectively, impartially, and inviolably, enjoyed and observed throughout our jurisdiction forever." The first and second declarations are as follows: —

"1st. No man's life shall be taken away, no man's honor or good name shall be stained, no man's person shall be arrested, restrained, banished, dismembered, nor any ways punished ; no man shall be deprived of his wife or children, no man's goods or estate shall be taken away from him, nor any way indamaged under color of law or countenance of authority, unless it be by virtue or equity of some express law of the country warranting the same, established by a General Court and sufficiently published, or in case of the defect of a law in any particular case, by the word of God. And in capital cases, or in cases concerning dismembering or banishment, according to that word to be judged by the General Court."

"2d. Every person within this jurisdiction, whether Inhabitant or foreigner, shall enjoy the same justice and law that is general for the plantation, which we constitute and execute one towards another, without partiality or delay."

In the face of this statute, Endicott being out of town, the deputy governor, Richard Bellingham, sent officers aboard the ship, who searched the baggage of these two passengers, and seized their books, which, by order of the authorities, were burned by the common executioner. The women were committed to prison, where they were confined for five weeks, when they were sent back to Barbadoes, the master of the ship being bound in one hundred pounds to take them there, and ordered not to suffer any to speak with them after they were put on board. It seems that while in gaol they used their own beds, which were brought out of the ship; these and their Bibles the gaoler confiscated to satisfy his fees. During their imprisonment no one was allowed to visit or to speak with them, and a board was nailed up before the window so that none might see them; they were denied all writing material, and no lights were permitted at night. They were so ill-fed or so starved, rather, that Nicholas Upsall, a church-member and freeman since 1631, bribed the gaoler with five shillings a week for the privilege of sending them provisions. Prior to this humane deed, he, or some other person whose heart had been touched by their sufferings, — it was probably Upsall, — had in vain offered to pay the five pounds penalty if permitted to visit the prisoners. As is usual with official despots, Bellingham made some show of legal procedure when this severe treatment was ordered. The council was convened, and a declaration issued, wherein it was said that "there are several laws long since made and published in this jurisdiction bearing testimony against heretics and erroneous persons," and that Ann Austin and Mary Fisher, " upon examination are found not only to be transgressors of the former laws, but to hold very dangerous, heretical, and blasphemous opinions; and they do also acknowledge that they came here purposely to propagate their said errors and heresies, bringing with them and spreading here sundry books, wherein are contained most corrupt, heretical, and blasphemous doctrines contrary to the truth of the gospel here professed amongst us. The council, therefore, tendering the preservation of the peace and truth enjoyed and professed among the churches of Christ in this country, do hereby order," etc. What very dangerous, heretical, and blasphemous opinions the prisoners held, we are left to surmise. Quaker authorities, however, furnish us a clew. They relate that one of the women said "thee," to Bellingham, whereupon he said, " he needed no more; now he knew they were Quakers." That little magic word was sufficient for the chief inquisitor. We are assured by one who should be excellent authority, that the people of Massachusetts were well informed as to the spirit and actings of the Quakers and were on the watch for them.[1] At last they had arrived. These two women, it was clear, were Quakers, and therefore they were heretics and blasphemers. It is to be observed that without any knowledge whatever of their opinions, their arrest was predetermined and they were imprisoned before they had spoken a word. They were not accused of crime, or misdemeanor, or with the utterance of heresy They were arrested, restrained, and finally banished, solely because they were Quakers and had intended to disseminate their opinions, if allowed to remain here. The magistrates proceeded under color of law, it is true, but none the less in violation of the fundamental law of the colony. However, we must not overlook the plea set up by some modern writers. The council, say these apologists, derived their authority from the royal charter. This document, after expressly providing that only such "orders, laws, ordinances, instructions, and directions aforesaid, not being repugnant to the laws and statutes of our realm of England," shall be promulgated, proceeds to invest the government

[1] *Massachusetts and its Early History*, p. 109.

with the war power. It provides "that it shall and may be lawful to and for the chief commanders, governors, and officers . . . for their special defense and safety, to encounter, expulse, repel, and resist by force of arms, as well by sea as by land, and by all fitting ways and means whatsoever, all such person and persons as shall at any time hereafter attempt or enterprise the destruction, invasion, detriment, or annoyance to the said plantation or inhabitants; and to take and surprise by all ways and means whatsoever, all and every such person and persons, with their ships, armor, munition, and other goods, as shall in hostile manner invade or attempt the defeating of the said plantation, or the hurt of the said company and inhabitants." We are assured that "through letters from friends at home," and their own familiarity with "the abounding pamphlets of religious controversy of these days," the Puritans were apprised of the dark designs of these two desperate and warlike Amazons, who in hostile bonnets and gowns had invaded Boston harbor. To be sure the Quaker books they brought with them gave the lie to the letters from England, but what need to read them? One of the dreadful women had said "thee" to the deputy governor, and her arrest prior to this *her* declaration of war was thus amply justified. The enemy had been surprised, "as well by sea as by land;" the invaders had been captured, and for a time, at least, the colony was safe. But could punishment too severe be meted out to such dangerous captives? John Endicott thought not; so he wrote a letter from Salem saying that had he been at home he would have had them well whipped. An ordeal far more terrible than scourging awaited them. By official order these two defenseless women were literally stripped of their clothing, and their bodies were examined for witch marks in a manner too indecent to be named.[1] If any one cares to know all that this implies, let him consult the Winthrop papers, vol. ii. p. 397, where he will find a narrative in detail of similar infliction upon the body of Margaret Jones, in the year 1648. The recital is too disgusting and sickening to be repeated. The treatment of that poor woman was inexcusable, but it was just and honorable as compared with the treatment of Ann Austin and Mary Fisher.

[1] *New England Judged*, p. 12.

Before Margaret Jones was arrested she had aroused the superstitious fears of the community. She had " a malignant touch, as many persons (men, women, and children) when she stroked . . . were taken with deafness . . . or sickness. She, practising physic, . . . her medicines were harmless, as anise-seed, liquors, etc., yet had extraordinary violent effects. . . . Some things which she foretold, came to pass accordingly." During her trial these alarming facts were duly proved to the jury, and she was found guilty of witchcraft and hanged for it. Governor Winthrop further narrates that "the same day and hour she was executed, there was a very great tempest at Connecticut which blew down many trees," etc. Though nothing can palliate the revolting torture to which she was subjected, nor justify the final punishment, it may be urged that in view of her practices a superstitious people might be pardoned for putting her under restraint. Her predictions, her stroking, and her potions had terrified the neighbors, and judging from the record, she was arrested and tried, in obedience to public sentiment. No such plea can be entered in the case of Ann Austin and Mary Fisher. They practiced no mysteries; they never had so much as a chance to speak to man, woman, or child of Boston; they were not transgressors of any law. There is nothing in the whole history of their case to relieve the blackness of the diabolical crime of which they were the victims. And yet a vice-president of the Massachusetts Historical Society tells us that the advent of the Quakers here began in "comedy"! On the contrary, the advent of the Quakers upon the soil of Massachusetts was marked by ghastly, grim tragedy far more terrible than the subsequent hanging of other Quakers, for it involved a living death, more to be dreaded than the gallows.

A few weeks after the enforced departure of Ann Austin and Mary Fisher, another vessel anchored in the harbor with nine Quakers aboard. They were immediately arrested and were imprisoned for about eleven weeks, when they were sent away in the ship that brought them, the master of the ship having been compelled by an arbitrary imprisonment to give security to take them to England at his own charge. The women were spared the shocking witchcraft ordeal, and apparently starvation was not attempted, but otherwise these Friends were subjected to the same severe treatment as their predecessors. During their confinement Governor Endicott bullied them with threats of hanging. "Take heed," he said to them, "ye break not our ecclesiastical laws, for then ye are sure to stretch by a halter." It was charged that they were guilty of " turbulent and contemptuous behavior to authority," but Bishop, a contemporary, whose integrity is not questioned by any one, pronounces this a " calumny forged out of your own and the brains of your priests." That it was a false charge is probable, for in the same Declaration, referring to Ann Austin, Mary Fisher, and these men and women, the authorities mendaciously assert that their " persons were only secured to be sent away the first opportunity, without censure or punishment." Without censure or punishment! The father of lies might well be staggered by such a shameless falsehood.

Early Friends, as has been shown, had profound respect for authority leavened with justice, but when officials degraded it and themselves by acts of cruel tyranny, they were prompt to resist and to rebuke. In the present case it is quite possible that some of the prisoners spoke their minds freely to their oppressors when opportunity offered. One of them, Mary Prince, it is alleged, saluted Endicott as he passed the gaol on his way to church, with such epithets as "vile oppressor," and " tyrant," and foretold that the Lord would " smite " him. It is also said that when the ministers interviewed her, she reproached them as " hirelings, Baal's priests," etc. Grant the correctness of these reports. Who does not honor the brave woman, the victim of Endicott's tyranny, for defying him with the simple truth? Who can censure her for refusing with contempt and righteous indignation the proffered offices of sanctimonious ministers who satirized the words of Jesus, " I was in prison, and ye came unto me," by visiting her to convict her of heresy and blasphemy, and with insufferable imperiousness to urge upon her the infallibility of their own superstitious dogmas?

The next act in this tragedy of errors was performed while these nine Quakers were still in gaol, but before any others had arrived and before any of the residents had avowed the Quaker name and faith. On the 14th day of October, 1656, the General Court enacted the first of a series of disgraceful laws, aimed exclusively at the Quakers.[1] It begins, " Whereas there is a cursed sect of heretics lately risen up in the world, which are commonly called Quakers," etc. This insulting vituperation is a fit inaugural to their bloody work, and aptly enough it is followed by monstrous calumny. Their victims have given them no cause for condemnation, and as they are the only Quakers with whom they have as yet dealt, they are forced, as we shall see, to trump up the alleged misdeeds of Friends in England, and to utilize the slanders culled from letters and controversial writings, in order to justify their charges. It is true that on another and later occasion they declare, " we were well assured by our own experience, as well as by the example of their predecessors in Munster," that it was the " design " of these prisoners " to undermine and ruin the peace and order " of the colony; but the assertion is an afterthought unsustained by evidence, and is as gross a

[1] See Appendix, p. 133.

calumny as the one with which it is coupled. The Quakers were as innocent of the Munster iniquities, which, by the way, occurred in the preceding century, as the Puritans themselves. The preamble to this law continues: "who take upon them to be immediately sent of God, and infallibly assisted by the Spirit to speak and write blasphemous opinions, despising government and the order of God in church and commonwealth, speaking evil of dignities, reproaching and reviling magistrates and ministers, seeking to turn the people from the faith and gain proselytes to their pernicious ways, this Court, taking into serious consideration the premises, and to prevent the like mischief as by their means is wrought in our native land, doth hereby order," etc. These calumnies are repeated under various forms in the text of subsequent laws, and were evidently relied upon to create a public sentiment that would justify the judicial crimes premeditated. After again denouncing the "blasphemous heretics," the law provides heavy penalties for ship-masters and others who may be convicted of bringing Quakers to the colony. Next, it is ordered, that Quakers coming within the jurisdiction "shall be forthwith committed to the house of correction, and at their entrance to be severely whipped, and by the master thereof be kept constantly to work, and none suffered to converse or speak with them during the time of their imprisonment, which shall be no longer than necessity requireth." Quaker books or " writings concerning their devilish opinions" are next interdicted, and persons who defend said books or opinions are fined, for the first offense forty shillings; for the second offense four pounds, and for the third offense they are first imprisoned and then banished. Lastly, it is " ordered, that what person or persons soever shall revile the office or person of magistrates or ministers, as is usual with the Quakers, such person or persons shall be severely whipped, or pay the sum of five pounds."

This formal declaration of war against the Quakers was proclaimed in the streets of Boston by beat of drum. Nicholas Upsall,[1] of whom mention has already been made, was proprietor of the Red Lyon Inn, and hearing the act read before his own door, said, " that he did look at it as a sad

[1] For biography see *The N. E. Historical and Genealogical Register* for January, 1880.

forerunner of some heavy judgment to fall on the country."

The authorities, hearing of this, quickly availed themselves of the opportunity to make perfectly clear what was meant by such terms as "reproaching honored magistrates." They summoned Upsall before the court the next morning, where he, "in much tenderness and love," warned them "to take heed lest ye should be found fighters against God." He was fined twenty pounds, Endicott saying, "I will not bate him one groat." He was then banished, with orders to depart in thirty days, four of which he spent in gaol, and before leaving he was fined three pounds more for not going to church.

On the 14th of October, 1657, a second law was enacted, the vituperation and reviling "usual" with the Puritan authorities being a prominent feature of the text. It provided for the forfeiture of one hundred pounds by any one who knowingly brought a Quaker into the jurisdiction, and imposed a fine of forty shillings for every hour's entainment of a Quaker by any resident. It further ordered that any Quaker man presuming to come into the jurisdiction after having once suffered what the law requireth, "shall for the first offense have one of his ears cut off . . . and for the second offense shall have his other ear cut off . . . and every woman Quaker that hath suffered the law here, that shall presume to come into this jurisdiction, shall be severely whipped . . . and so also for her coming again she shall be alike used as aforesaid; and for every Quaker, he or she, that shall a third time herein again offend, they shall have their tongues bored through with a hot iron. . . . And it is further ordered that all and every Quaker arising from amongst ourselves shall be dealt with and suffer the like punishment as the law provides against foreign Quakers." [1]

On the 19th of May, 1658, for a third time the General Court issued its decree against the Friends, forbidding, under severe penalties, the holding of meetings or attendance at meetings. This law, also, is well flavored with the usual reviling and calumny.[2]

On the 19th of October, 1658, the Court enacted the fourth law, in which they incorporated Endicott's threat, " take heed ye

[1] See Appendix, p. 136.   [2] See Appendix, p. 137.

break not our ecclesiastical laws, for then ye are sure to stretch by the halter." The preamble not only recites the old list of calumnies, but lengthens it with fresh slanders. It is followed by an order banishing both visiting and resident Quakers upon pain of death if they return. Very properly this order is amply padded with Puritan railing and abuse.

On May 11, 1659, by a special order, the county treasurers were authorized to sell Daniel and Provided Southwicke, son and daughter to Lawrence Southwicke,[1] to any of the English nation at Virginia or Barbadoes, to satisfy the fines imposed upon them "for siding with the Quakers and absenting themselves from the public ordinances."[2]

Edmund Batter, the treasurer of Salem, undertook to carry out this order. He was a foul-mouthed villain who reveled in assaults upon defenseless men and women, and who was never so happy as when engaged in hunting down the Quakers. Pages might be filled with a recital of his infamous deeds as they are recounted by Bishop, but he shall speak for himself, as

[1] See Appendix, p. 174. [2] See Appendix, p. 175.

his own recorded confession sufficiently indicates his character. It may prove an instructive study to those modern writers who note every expression of righteous indignation uttered by the Quakers, and roll it as a sweet morsel under the tongue, meanwhile remembering to forget the invective and railing of the Puritans.

In the unpublished county court records at Salem, there is the following entry under date " 26th 4mo. 1660." " Mr. Edmund Batter being presented to this Court for saying that Elizabeth Kitchin had been a pawawing and calling her base quaking slutt with divers other oprobious and taunting speeches, the presentment being not fully proved (he confest that he said to the said Elizabeth) either have you beene, or she had beene a pawawing and did say to her she was a quaking slutt (meeting of her betimes in the morning comeing as he supposed from a quaker meeting, seeing also som other persons that waies afected) comeing that waye which she came, is by the Court admonished and to pay fees of Court 30s."

Innocent women were stripped to the waist and thus exposed to public gaze, were beaten with stripes until the blood ran down their bare backs and bosoms; the ears of men were cut off and the bodies of men were beaten to a jelly, for attending Quaker meetings and for testifying against "your bloody and cruel laws;" but cowardly bullies and blackguards, such as Edmund Batter, when they insulted Quaker women, were only admonished and obliged to pay court fees; nor did their indecency prevent their being honored church-members and trusted officials in the Puritan commonwealth, which we are taught to believe was, *par excellence*, the stronghold of piety and morality.

This Edmund Batter hunted in vain for a ship-master mean enough to sail freighted with human victims for a Virginia market. One captain, being approached, "to try Batter, said,—that they would spoil all the vessel's company," whereupon he replied, with a testimony to the inoffensive character of the Quakers, rarely extorted from Puritan lips. He said to the ship-captain, "Oh, you need not fear that, for they are poor harmless creatures and will not hurt anybody." "Will they not so? (said the ship-master) and will ye offer to make slaves of so harmless creatures?" Whittier has immortalized this scene by rendering the captain's answer in the following lines: —

"Pile my ship with bars of silver, — pack with coins of Spanish gold,
From keel-piece up to deck-plank, the roomage of her hold,
By the living God who made me! — I would sooner in your bay
Sink ship and crew and cargo, than bear this child away!"

On the 22d of May, 1661, finding the hanging business had been somewhat overdone, the Court, with the customary calumny and vindictive epithet, enacted a new statute, wherein it is ordered that Quakers, both men and women, are to "be stripped naked from the middle upwards, and tied to a cart's tail and whipped through the town;" also to "be branded with the letter R on their left shoulder," and "the constables of the several towns are empowered . . . to impress cart, oxen, and other assistance for the execution of this order."[1] The author of "The New England Tragedies in Prose" probably wrote his

[1] See Appendix, p. 141. The persistent slander of the Quakers is well illustrated by the terms of this law, in which the Friends are described as "vagabonds." The history of Friends, the world over, from the rise of the Society down to the present day, does not afford a single instance of Quaker pauperism or vagrancy. Neither the Colony nor the State of Massachusetts was ever asked to spend one shilling for the benefit of a Quaker.

narrative under the full conviction that his
treatment of the Quakers is very magnan-
imous, and his criticism of the Puritans
sufficiently severe; but in common with
several other apologists, he manifests an
ignorance concerning the real mission and
character of the Quakers, combined with
an acquired or hereditary bias in favor of
the Puritans, by which he is emphatically
disqualified for rendering impartial judgment. In alluding to the passage and the
enforcement of the inhuman law, of which
the pivotal sentence has just been quoted,
he says, with unconscious irony, "as the
clemency of the rulers began its gentler
sway, for a time, at least, the vehemence
of the disturbers seemed to increase." A
Daniel come to judgment! Adopting the
prejudiced opinions of the historian Palfrey,
he believes that "seldom have enthusiasts
been more coarse, more unfriendly, more
wild and annoying than the early Friends."
His sympathy for the persecuted Puritans
is so aroused that, for the moment, the
spirit of old John Norton seems to possess
him. With the vision of an innocent woman stripped to the waist, hauled from town
to town, and flogged as she is dragged along

at the cart's tail, — with this brutal sight in his mind's eye, he commends "the clemency of the rulers," and, with implied surprise, notes that under its " gentler sway " the vehemence of the disturbers seemed to increase. Such wretched twaddle is more than discreditable. It is puerile; and yet it passes for historical criticism.

On the 27th of November, 1661, in obedience to an order from Charles II., King of England, to whom the Friends had applied for relief, the Court ordered "that the execution of the laws in force against Quakers, as such, so far as they respect corporal punishment or death, be suspended until this court take further order;"[1] but on the 8th of October, 1662, their fear of the King being allayed, they reënacted the law of May, 1661, with an amendment providing that " the whipping be but through three towns; and the magistrates . . . shall appoint both the towns and the number of the stripes in each town to be given."

[1] For this famous " King's Missive," and brief comment, see Appendix, pp. 188-191.

CHAPTER III.

THE WARFARE.

WE have now passed in review the Puritan legislation against the Quakers during the six years of the reign of terror.[1] The story of its vigorous enforcement stains the saddest page of our early history, — not even excepting the witchcraft delusion, that, at a later day, swept through the colony. Incredible as the narration seems to us, no one suspects that the sufferers or the Quaker historians are guilty of exaggeration.

The tongue boring and the branding penalties were not resorted to in this colony,[2] but three victims had their right ears cut off, and four suffered the death penalty. The number of homes broken up by banishment and the extent of the impoverishment of families by confiscation of property have yet to be computed. Nor is it known how many

[1] For subsequent legislation, etc., see Appendix, pp. 191, 192.

[2] In the New Haven Colony, Humphrey Norton was branded " H " (Heresy) in the hand.

scourgings were inflicted. Dr. Ellis thinks that about thirty victims had suffered whippings by order of the General Court alone, and many more from local courts, *prior* to the passage of the "vagabond law" in May, 1661, and it is well known that a carnival of cruelty followed the enactment of that law.

To the credit of the people of the colony it should be said that the passage of these laws and their merciless enforcement were not sustained by public opinion. It is true that in October, 1658, a petition,[1] signed by twenty-five citizens, asked for severer laws against the Quakers, but there is good reason for believing that it was instigated by John Norton and other ministers. It did not represent the sentiments of the community. Remembering the fate of Nicholas Upsall, it would have been hazardous for any one to circulate or present a counter petition; nevertheless, there were times when public indignation was with difficulty restrained from manifesting itself by open revolt. This was notably true in the early part of 1658, when the barbarous treatment of William Brend by his gaoler was noised

[1] See Appendix, p. 153.

abroad. To quell the rising turmoil, and to appease an exasperated people, the authorities publicly promised to punish the gaoler; but Brend, whose life for a time hung by a thread, recovered, and the tumult subsiding, the insincerity of the magistrates was revealed. Their promise was broken, the gaoler retained his office, and his barbarity was applauded by pious John Norton.

The law ordering banishment upon pain of death had been passed with difficulty, and by a bare majority of one vote.

In October, 1659, when William Robinson, Marmaduke Stevenson, and Mary Dyer were sentenced to death, military precautions were taken to prevent an outbreak. A conception of the fears of the magistrates and the excitement of the populace is possible, when we remember that the population of Boston was, at the most, but a few thousands; and then read in the official record that the prisoners were escorted to the gallows by "Captain James Oliver, with one hundred soldiers, completely armed with pike, and musketeers, with powder and bullet." A drummer marched in advance of the condemned prisoners, and when either of them attempted to speak, the drum was beaten. During the execution thirty-six soldiers were posted about the town as sentinels, to preserve the peace. Prior to the execution it was "ordered that the selectmen of Boston shall . . . press ten or twelve able and faithful persons, every night during the sitting of this court, to watch with great care the town, especially the prison," etc. Evidently a rescue was feared. At the same sitting of the court two declarations were issued. One of them is a long document largely devoted to a scriptural refutation of Quaker doctrines.[1] The other is mainly composed of a string of calumnies designed to inflame the people against the Friends. Both of them appeal to the religious prejudices and bigotry of the colony, and were evidently published under the fear of righteous retribution by an outraged community. Even stern John Endicott scented danger, and hastened to vindicate the court from "the clamorous accusation of severity."

The authorities professed that they were reluctant to execute the Quakers, and it is true that at the solicitation of her son a

[1] See Appendix, pp. 143-152.

60   THE QUAKER INVASION

reprieve was granted to Mary Dyer, by which her life was spared, only to be taken, however, upon her subsequent visit to the colony. It is very evident that they were determined to make an example of Robinson and Stevenson, for they turned a deaf ear to the earnest entreaties of their more enlightened neighbors. John Winthrop, Governor of Connecticut, said he would beg them on his bare knees not to execute the law; and Colonel Temple said to the court that if they really "desired their lives absent rather than their deaths present, he would beg them of you, and carry them away at his own charge . . . and if any of them should come amongst ye again he would again fetch them at his own charge."[1] This proposition was favorably received by most of the magistrates; but the stronger wills of a few leading officials overcame all opposition, and the order for the execution was confirmed.

When Wenlock Christison, who is erroneously represented as having recanted,[2] was

[1] *New England Judged*, pp. 157–158.
[2] See *The Memorial History of Boston*, p. 187. A facsimile of Christison's letter is given on page 188. "I, the condemned man, do give forth under my hand, that if I may have my liberty I have freedom to depart this jurisdiction,

convicted, the court deliberated for two weeks before a verdict of guilty was obtained. Even then it was only through the indomitable will of Endicott that a sentence of death was secured. His more humane comrades faltered, hesitating to add another judicial murder to their list of crimes, whereupon Endicott lost his temper, and,

and I know not that ever I shall come into it any more." By "freedom to depart," a mode of expression which is peculiar to Friends even at the present day, the prisoner undoubtedly meant that having obeyed the call of sacred duty by coming here and testifying against the murder of his friend William Leddra (who had been executed in March, 1661), nothing further was required of him at the time. He had no vainglorious wish to suffer martyrdom, but was subject to the will of the Lord, and would lay down his life when it was required of him. What the Divine leading might be hereafter, he could not foretell. If it took him to Boston, the magistrates would see him again, but if not, he had no desire to renew their acquaintance. Instead of "showing the white feather," as the Rev. Mr. Dexter sneeringly puts it in his book, *As to Roger Williams*, Christison was courageously faithful to duty as it was revealed to him. For such a man it was harder to retreat and by so doing subject himself to the charge of cowardice, than it was to face death. His whole life, so far as it is known, sustains this theory. The fact that he did return into the jurisdiction and suffer further violence from the hands of the same officials is sufficient refutation of the charge of recantation so carelessly made by several writers. Had he obtained his release by a promise not to return, the promise would have been kept, for in spite of an exaggerated manner of speech charged upon the early Friends, even their most bitter detractors will concede that their word was as inviolate as the judicial oaths of other men.

flinging something furiously upon the table, wished himself back in England, and said, "You that will not consent, record it; I thank God I am not afraid to give judgment;" he then, amid confusion, "precipitately pronounced judgment himself." This impetuous and relentless inquisitor was eventually obliged to stay his hand from further murder, and to satisfy his craving for Quaker blood by drawing it from the backs and breasts of helpless women.[1]

The story of William Brend's sufferings, as related by Sewel, admirably illustrates the extreme cruelty of the officials, the unyielding determination of the authorities, and the disapproving public sentiment that extensively prevailed. He says: "In the latter part of the Fifth month, [1658], it came to pass, that William Brend and William Leddra, having been at Salem, came to Newbury; where at the house of one Robert Adams they had a conference with the priest, in the presence of Captain Gerish, who had promised that they should not suffer; but after the conference was ended, the captain would not let them go, but on prom-

[1] When the executioner whipped Ann Coleman "he split the nipple of her breast, which so tortured her that it had almost cost her life." *New England Judged*, p. 430.

ise presently to depart the town; which being loth to comply with, as they were on their way, they were sent for back, and Captain Gerish riding after them, commanded them to return; which they refusing, he compelled them thereunto, and sent them with a constable to Salem; where, being brought before the magistrates, they were asked 'whether they were Quakers?' to which they answered, 'that they were such that were in scorn called so.' Next it was objected to them 'that they maintained dangerous errors.' They asking what these errors were, it was told them, 'that they not only denied that Christ at Jerusalem had suffered on the cross, but also that they denied the Holy Scriptures.' They boldly contradicted this, and said 'they owned no other Jesus but he that had suffered death at Jerusalem, and that they also owned the Scriptures.' Now although nothing could be objected against this, yet they were carried to the house of correction, as such who, according to the law made at Boston, might not come into those parts. Some days after they were carried to Boston, where in the next month they were brought into the house of correction to work there. But they, unwilling to submit thereto, the gaoler, who sought his profit from the work of his prisoners, would not give them victuals, though they offered to pay for them. But he told them ' it was not their money but their labor he desired.' Thus he kept them five days without food, and then with a three-corded whip gave them twenty blows. An hour after he told them ' they might go out, if they would pay the marshal that was to lead them out of the country.' They judging it very unreasonable to pay money for being banished, refused this, but yet said ' that if the prison-door was set open, they would go away.' The next day the gaoler came to Wm. Brend, a man in years, and put him in irons, neck and heels so close together, that there was no more room left between each, than for the lock that fastened them. Thus he kept him from five in the morning till after nine at night, being the space of sixteen hours. The next morning he brought him to the mill to work, but Brend refusing, the gaoler took a pitched rope about an inch thick, and gave him twenty blows over his back and arms, with as much force as he could, so that the rope untwisted, and then going away, he came again with another rope that was thicker and stronger, and told Brend, ' that he would cause him to bow to the law of the country, and make him work.' Brend judged this not only unreasonable in the highest degree, since he had committed no evil, but he was also altogether unable to work; for he wanted strength for want of food, having been kept five days without eating, and whipped also, and now thus unmercifully beaten with a rope. But this inhuman gaoler relented not, but began to beat anew with his pitched rope on this bruised body, and foaming at his mouth like a madman, with violence laid four-score and seventeen blows more on him, as other prisoners, that beheld it with compassion, have told; and if his strength and his rope had not failed him, he would have laid on more; he threatened also to give him the next morning as many blows more. But a higher power, who sets limits even to the raging sea, and hath said, ' Hitherto shalt thou come, but no further,' also limited this butcherly fellow, who was yet impudently stout enough to say his morning-prayer. To what a most terrible condition these blows brought the body of Brend, (who because of the great heat of the weather, had nothing but a serge cassock upon his shirt) may easily be conceived; his back and arms were bruised and black, and the blood hanging as in bags under his arms; and so into one was his flesh beaten, that the sign of a particular blow could not be seen; for all was become as a jelly. His body being thus cruelly tortured, he lay down upon the boards, so extremely weakened, that the natural parts decaying, and strength quite failing, his body turned cold: there seemed as it were a struggle between life and death; his senses were stopped, and he had for some time neither seeing, feeling, nor hearing, till at length, a divine power prevailing, life broke through death, and the breath of the Lord was breathed into his nostrils. Now the noise of this cruelty spread among the people in the town, and caused such a cry, that the governor sent his surgeon to the prison, to see what might be done; but the surgeon found the body of Brend in such a deplorable condition, that, as one without hopes, he said, 'his flesh would rot from off his bones, ere the bruised parts could be brought to digest.' This so exasperated the people that the magistrates, to prevent a tumult, set up a paper on their meeting-house door, and up and down the streets, as it were to show their dislike of this abominable and most barbarous cruelty; and said, the gaoler should be dealt withal the next court. But this paper was soon taken down again upon the instigation of the high priest, John Norton, who having from the beginning been a fierce promoter of the persecution, now did not stick to say, 'W. Brend endeavored to beat our gospel-ordinances black and blue; if he then be beaten black and blue, it is but just upon him; and I will appear in his behalf that did so.' It is therefore not much to be wondered at, that these precise and bigoted magistrates, who would be looked upon to be eminent for piety, were so cruel in persecuting, since their chief teacher thus wickedly encouraged them to it."

Further evidence of the advanced civilization of the people, as contrasted with the inhumanity of the ministers and magistrates, might be cited, but as this fact is generally conceded, even by very partisan writers, it is unnecessary to pursue the subject further. It may be well to suggest, however, that had the right of suffrage been extended to all citizens of character and good repute, instead of being limited to church-members, it is probable there would have been an infusion of true religion and humanity into the laws, and the colony would have been spared the tragic record which now mars its history.

CHAPTER IV.

CHARACTER AND CONDUCT OF THE INVADERS.—
MODERN REVIEWERS REVIEWED.

THERE are some facts and more fancies in which popular writers believe they find not only the *casus belli* between the Puritans and Quakers, but also great palliation and partial justification for the persecution involved therein. At the outset we are met with the assertion that the Quakers had no right to come here, and that the right to prohibit their coming was complete. The simple act of entrance into the colony, regardless of the object of the visit, it is alleged, was an aggravated assault upon the Puritan homestead.

This theory, first propounded by the Puritans themselves, has come to be accepted as historical truth, and no one of our prominent writers has thought it important to state that the Quakers denied it with as much emphasis, and with at least as great sincerity, as the Puritans asserted it. The

Quakers claimed that as Englishmen they had the legal right to visit or to live wherever the English flag proclaimed English jurisdiction.[1] This claim rested upon that clause in the charter which expressly guaranties "all liberties and immunities of free and natural subjects of . . . the realm," to all Englishmen "which shall go to and inhabit" Massachusetts, or "which shall happen to be born there, or on the seas in going thither or returning from thence."[2] The authorities relied upon the same charter, in which they professed to find warrant to build a Chinese wall around the colony. Now the only clause of the charter that can be used to justify such arbitrary legislation is the one already quoted, and which, as we have seen, is a grant of the war power to the colonial government, and nothing more. Legal quibbling was apparently as easy then as now, and the charter, wrested from its purpose, was made an instrument of tyranny. But if the Puritans quibbled, their apologists do something worse when they justify the treatment of the Quakers on the pretense that they had no business here,

---

[1] See Bishop and other early Quaker historians.
[2] *Massachusetts Records,* vol. i. p. 16.

and that, by coming, they forfeited their rights; for the fact is, that four fifths of them were residents of the colony, and were recognized as such by the authorities long before the persecution began. Upsall, Southwick, and others were freemen. The Buffums, Whartons, Shattucks, and scores of others, were property holders and reputable citizens.[1] Hereafter when the coming of the Quakers is under discussion, in the interest of justice let this fact be remembered, and let it not be forgotten, that these people bravely maintained what they believed to be their chartered rights. They appealed, also, to the "Body of the Liberties," previously referred to, wherein they found ample guaranty of protection for both residents and strangers. Paper guaranties, it is true, availed them nothing; but they are of essential value to us when judgment is to be rendered. Sooner or later, the opinion now popular with historians must be reversed, and the claim of the Quakers, both to come and to live here, will be sustained.

[1] Samuel Winthrop, a son of Governor Winthrop, was a Quaker. He does not figure in the Quaker annals of Massachusetts, but was a resident and a leading citizen of Antigua,

But the main charge in the indictment of the Quakers, and the one upon which Puritan apologists most rely to justify their own clients, is that Quakerism manifested itself here in the persistent and frequent lawlessness and indecent conduct of its adherents. We are taught to believe that the Puritans were exasperated beyond endurance, and that the solution of Puritan persecution is to be found in the extravagances of the Friends. Will this plea bear the test of examination?

In the first place, it is to be remarked that many writers accept this convenient solution, and recount the story as told by prejudiced authorities, while others rake the records, and, without caring to test their correctness, parade every instance of misdemeanor that they find charged upon the Friends, with relentless fidelity to the purpose of their search. In Grahame's History it is related that one Faubord attempted to imitate Abraham, and was only prevented from sacrificing his son by the interference of his neighbors. This story is copied by a later writer and handed down as a speci-

where he bravely maintained the principles and testimonies of Friends. Besse, vol. ii. chap. ix. p. 371.

men of a Quaker's "blasphemous atrocity."[1] Now to the mind of any one who has even slight knowledge of Quaker doctrines the account in itself convicts its author of malicious slander, for the Friends maintained unqualifiedly that the old dispensation had been superseded by the gospel of Jesus, and that outward sacrifice was an abomination.

One of the foulest calumnies that disgrace the pages of history is perpetuated by the Rev. Henry M. Dexter,[2] who reproduces a story told by Increase Mather, to the effect that two Quaker women and a man named Dunen danced naked together. One of the women, Mary Ross, said she was Christ, and commanded Dunen, whom she called the Apostle Peter, to sacrifice a dog. There is more of similar stuff which need not be repeated. After the recital, the reverend editor, probably to shield himself from the charge of willful misrepresentation, concedes that " the better sort of the new sect by this time had begun to repudiate such excesses ;" but, he adds, " the sober

[1] R. H. Allen, in *The New England Tragedies in Prose*, p. 51.
[2] *As to Roger Williams*, pp. 124-141.

portion of the population of New England" found it "difficult to draw the line between 'Old' and 'New Quakers.'" This libel upon the Friends was exposed by one of them, a contemporary, who wrote a book in answer to the "calumnies, lies and abuses" heaped upon the Friends by Cotton Mather, who repeats the story. Referring to this particular calumny and to others, he says, "our adversaries . . . rake up such dirty stories to throw at us," and these "mad pranks no more concern the Quakers . . . than they do the Presbyterians."[1] But the extent of the meanness of this attempt by Mr. Dexter to dishonor the early Friends is the more fully realized when he is found characterizing them, in the same book, as "mild and peaceful."[2] This he does when he quotes their condemnation of Roger Williams for the purpose of justifying his own aspersion of Williams's character. The attack upon early Friends by Hon. Joel Parker,[3] published by the Massachu-

[1] *Truth and Innocency Defended*, pp. 129–132. Bound in one volume with *New England Judged*. Edition of 1702.

[2] *As to Roger Williams*, p. 82.

[3] This ingenious lawyer describes the Quakers as "the nuisance" of the colony, and proves (to his own satisfaction) that they were *not persecuted* by the Puritan authorities.

setts Historical Society, is a master-piece of partisan pleading; but the unfairness of Mr. Dexter in his entire treatment of the Quakers exceeds even that of Parker.

The "Magnalia"[1] of Cotton Mather is a storehouse of ammunition for apologists; and writers who would not willingly do injustice are sometimes betrayed into misrepresentation by consulting it and forgetting to consult Quaker histories. A striking example of this may be found in an article by Mr. John Fiske of Cambridge, published in "Harper's Monthly Magazine" for December, 1882. In this article Mr. Fiske adopts the popular view of the merits of the conflict waged between the Puritans and Quakers, apparently without having examined the pages of a single Quaker authority, and enlivens it with the addition of Cotton Mather's statement, that the Friends called the Bible the "Word of the Devil." A slight familiarity with this branch of his subject would have been sufficient to prevent Mr. Fiske from marring his entertaining and instructive paper by the introduction of a stale calumny which even

[1] Book vii. chap. iv. The Quakers are called "devil driven creatures" and "dangerous villains."

partisan commentators have not had the presumption to renew, and which has been refuted by every Quaker writer who mentions the Bible, and specifically by a contemporaneous authority. In his review of Mather's charges, written soon after they were made, John Whiting says, "And as to any Quakers, whom he calls wretches, ordinarily saying among the people, we deny thy Christ; we deny thy God, which thou callest Father Son, and Spirit; *thy Bible is the Word of the Devil;* both these charges we utterly deny, as false in fact, and challenge him to prove who or when any Quaker said so; and if any ever did or do, we should disown it and testify against them; for we abhor the very thoughts of any such expressions."[1] Friend Whiting's challenge, it need not be said, was never answered. As the case stands, Mr. Fiske has revived and extensively published a slanderous falsehood. But Mather, it should be said, has excellent indorsement which Mr. Fiske may have seen. If not, he can find it in the Diary of Judge Sewall, recently published, wherein the Puritan judge seriously defines Quakerism as "Devil worship." It

---

[1] *Truth and Innocency Defended*, p. 89.

will be easy now to construct a new justification of the Puritans, for what more natural than for a people who worshiped the Devil, and accepted the Bible as the inspired word, to maintain that the Devil wrote it? This important theory being conclusively established by the corroborative testimony of two pious and truthful Puritans, one can only marvel at the forbearance of the colonial ministers and magistrates.

In justice to Mr. Fiske it must be admitted that he is not singular in his methods of research; for with rare exceptions every modern history of this subject confirms the suspicion that when early authorities have been consulted at all, it has been for the sole purpose of confirming preconceived opinions, and for the selection of material to be used in extenuating the crimes of John Endicott, John Norton, and their associates. A notable illustration of the slip-shod method of some writers who aspire to become historians is furnished by Mr. H. C. Lodge. He says the Friends were drunk with religious zeal. He evidently believes that it was not unusual for them to appear naked in public, and he describes them as rioters and disturbers of the peace.[1] The "presentation of facts" which he professes to give is a mere rehash of some of the worst and most abusive attacks upon the Quakers by older writers and has no proper claim to be called historical. In the preface to his book, Mr. Lodge innocently assures the reader that he makes "absolutely no pretense to original research." *Cela va sans dire.*

Of the many apologists who essay to deal with this subject, the Rev. Dr. George E. Ellis is probably the best informed; and if he could but address himself to the matter with a mind free from the apparently inevitable New England prejudice, he might do history important service by correcting the errors of his predecessors. He finds something to admire in Quakers and Quakerism, and something to condemn in Puritans and Puritanism. His judgments are not always consistent, and they sometimes positively conflict with each other, but in their general tenor and bearing they coincide with the conclusions and judgments of other apologists. The main difference is, that while such critics as Parker and

[1] *A Short History of the English Colonies in America*, p. 354.

Dexter indulge in wholesale condemnation of the Friends, Dr. Ellis's verdict is relieved by some recognition of the Quaker virtues and by a recommendation of mercy. He concedes that " the Quakers had hold in common of an advanced truth, quick with the energy of the Spirit." He grants that " they were the advanced pleaders for a liberty which is now our life, for a form of faith and piety which alone has power for a free soul." He " can apprehend the high and pure motive which not only led, but really inspired these unwelcome missionaries to our bay." He pays a tribute to their " sincerity " and to their " meek, but always unflinching endurance of contumely and violence." He even admits that " much of their terrible abusiveness of language was wholly free from malice and any ill-intention, but was prompted wholly from an honest and severely righteous sense of the errors and superstitions which they assailed."

It is not easy for the ordinary mind to understand how a people, confessedly governed by a sense of religious duty and led and inspired to come here by a high and pure motive, were at the same time impelled by an "aimless spirit of annoyance," or that, " by every rule of right and reason, they ought to have kept away." Nor is it less difficult to realize that the pleaders for a form of faith and piety which alone has power for a free soul uttered, " in a prophetical way," " crude and indigested notions " that " sounded like the wildest rant," to be relieved of the reproach of blasphemy only by being referred to " a besotted stupidity or a shade of distraction." There is a sharp contrast, if not flat contradiction, between the portraiture of the Friends, as we have just seen it, and the following sketch, drawn by the same hand. The Quakers, says Dr. Ellis, were " seditious and rancorous visitors," and " most of them " were " lawless and ignorant." They were " intrusive, pestering, indecent, and railing disturbers of early Massachusetts," who " regarded themselves as led by the Spirit to give 'testimony,' which, as things then were, would subvert all civil and religious order in this colony, and overwhelm it with confusion and anarchy. . . . A spell wrought upon their spirits, and they yielded themselves, as they thought, to a guidance from above. . . . Modest and pure women under this spell would rush into the public highways, or into a crowded place of worship, and, independent of all the art or materials of dressmakers, would make a distressing spectacle of themselves. One such, coming into a meeting-house in this condition, had smeared herself with black paint as a sign, she said, of the black pox, which, she prophesied, God would send on this cruel jurisdiction." This graphic picture is drawn for our contemplation in order to " relieve the burden of wanton and ruthless cruelty cast upon our legislators," who were " beyond measure provoked and goaded to the course which they pursued. . . . Their Quaker tormentors were the aggressive party ; they wantonly initiated the strife, and with dogged pertinacity persisted in outrages which drove the authorities almost to frenzy. . . . Our Fathers cared little, if at all, for the Quaker theology. They did not get so far as that in dealing with them. . . . Our Fathers dealt with them on the score of their manners, their lawlessness, and their offensive speech and behavior."

It is inconceivable how an artist can produce two such irreconcilable pictures as these with but one subject for his model, and it must be left to Philip sober and Philip drunk to settle their own differences.[1] The substance of Dr. Ellis's diatribe against the Friends is reproduced here, because, as has been said, it is an epitome of current misconception, and because the main argument used to justify the Puritans rests upon this misconception. The aim and purpose of Dr. Ellis is to portray the conditions under which the Puritans were "goaded," and thus to account for "the course which they pursued." In opposition to his view of the subject, three statements or propositions are offered for the consideration of the reader.

First. The testimonies of the Quakers were not blasphemous, nor do they indicate "a besotted stupidity or a shade of distraction." On the contrary, they were fervently religious, and were often marked by a vigorous understanding that would do credit even to some of the wise men of our own generation. Much of their testimony, had it been heeded, would have strengthened the civil and religious order of the

---

[1] For what Dr. Ellis has written about the Quakers, see *Massachusetts and its Early History; The Memorial History of Boston*, vol. i.; and *Proceedings of the Massachusetts Historical Society*, vol. xviii.

colony. They testified in behalf of a religious and social order that grows out of an intelligent and just administration of an enlightened government. Dr. Ellis has superior facilities for historical investigation, and no doubt holds in reserve much valuable information accumulated during many years of arduous study. If he has evidence to sustain his cruel characterization of the testimony of the Friends he ought to publish it. Such reports as are ordinarily accessible do not warrant his accusation ; and until he makes it good by substantial and conclusive proof, one is obliged to suspect that he has carelessly adopted the unsustained charges of some earlier writer.

The sermons of the Quakers were never written nor reported ; but there are letters addressed to the authorities, now on file with the court records, and also other letters printed in Friends' journals and histories, which not only reveal the religious and mental character and the views of the writers, but may also fairly be relied upon to indicate some of the prevailing Quaker opinions, both as to ecclesiastical and civil law. A fac-simile of the signatures of two Quaker women to one of these letters is printed on page 185 of " The Memorial History of Boston." The letter is addressed " To thee John Indicott and the rest of the rulers of this jurisdiction." The editor calls it " a characteristic letter," and one therefore naturally expects to find it irreligious, where it does not betoken " a besotted stupidity or a shade of distraction." So far from this, a profoundly religious feeling pervades the whole letter, and the unsparing scriptural denunciation is relieved by a tenderness and pathos that free the writers from all suspicion of malice. The women were evidently of ordinary education, for their style is not only quaint, but often obscure. It must be remembered, however, that the writing of even literary men in those days was prolix and redundant, and much of it must be reconstructed in order to be made perfectly clear and readily intelligible to the modern eye and ear. The spirit of this letter may be judged from the following abstract : —

" We can rejoice that we are counted worthy and called hereunto to bear our testimony against a cruel and hard-hearted people who are slighting the day of your visitation and foolishly requiting the Lord for his goodness and shamefully intreating his hidden ones whom he has sent amongst you to call you from the evil of your ways. . . . The Lord our God is arising as a mighty and terrible one to plead the cause of his people and to clear the cause of the innocent: but surely he will in no wise acquit the guilty who have shed the blood of the innocent and ye shall assuredly feel his judgment. . . . Woe, woe unto you for you have forsaken the Lord, the fountain of living water, and are greedily swallowing the polluted waters that come through the stinking [1] channel of your howling master's unclean spirits; whom Christ cries woe against and who cannot cease from sin, having hearts exercised with covetous practices: woe unto them (saith the Scriptures) for they have run greedily after the error of Balaam who loved the wages of unrighteousness. . . .

" Surely the overflowing scourge will pass over you and sweep away your refuge of lies and your covenant with hell shall be disannulled. . . . Oh that you had owned the day of your visitation before it had been

[1] This old English word, now almost obsolete except in vulgar circles, was familiar to polite ears and in frequent use in the seventeenth century. See quotation from Milton, p. 12; and from Rev. John Higginson, p. 95.

too late and had hearkened to the voice of his servants whom he hath sent unto you again and again in love and tenderness to yourselves. . . . And then these wicked laws had never been made nor prosecuted. . . . Your glorying will be turned into shame and confusion of face and your beauty will be as a fading flower which suddenly withereth away. . . . We have written to clear our conscience, and if you should account us your enemies for speaking the truth, and heat the furnace of our affliction hotter, yet know we shall not fall down and worship your wills ; . . . all the sufferings that we have endured (from you) for Christ, have not at all marred his visage to us, but we still see more beauty in him ; well knowing that as they did unto him so they will do unto us, and now they are come to pass, we remember that he said these things. MARY TRASK,
MARGARET SMITH.

"From your house of correction where we have been unjustly restrained from our children and habitations, one of us above ten months and the other about eight ; and where we are yet continued by your oppressors that know no shame. Boston, 21st of ye 10^{mth}, 1660."

When Wenlock Christison was on trial for his life, he said to the court, "Do not think to weary out the living God by taking away the lives of his servants! What do you gain by it? For the last man that you put to death, here are five come in his room: and if you have power to take my life from me, God can raise up the same principle of life in ten of his servants and send them among you, in my room, that you may have torment upon torment, which is your portion; for there is no peace to the wicked, saith my God."

The righteous indignation of this heroic soul is sometimes referred to as evidence of a malicious spirit. Does it not rather show the spirit of a martyr who, in the hour of peril, was faithful to the memory of his murdered friends and dared to confront their executioners with uncompromising fidelity to the cause for which they died?

John Burstow was one of the five Friends referred to by Christison, who had come into the presence of the court to support him in the hour of trial. But little is known of him beyond this fact, and that while in gaol, in 1661, he wrote a letter to his persecutors in which he expresses his belief that their hearts were hardened beyond redemption, and that the righteous judgments of the Lord would be poured forth upon them. His letter is unmistakably that of a Puritan who, having been converted to Quakerism, nevertheless continued to draw his inspiration mainly from the old Hebrew prophets. A few sentences will give the spirit of the letter, which, however denunciatory it may be, is neither blasphemous nor stupid. "Your assemblies are an abomination to the Lord, your hands are defiled with blood . . . ye that have an ear to hear, hearken and come forth from among them that ye may be as fire-brands plucked out of the fire, for as certainly as the plagues were poured forth upon hard-hearted Pharaoh, shall the plagues and judgments of the Lord be poured forth upon the inhabitants of this town of Boston."

Josiah Southwick was a representative Quaker. A full recital of his sufferings would melt a heart of stone, and yet he addressed a letter, from the gaol, to the General Court, of which the following is an extract. It fitly indicates the spirit of the entire letter: "Some have said we are the persecutors, but we know we are the persecuted: yet we can freely say, the Lord lay not your sin to your charge, for I believe many of you know not what you do."

During her imprisonment, Mary Dyer addressed a letter to the "General Court at Boston," in which she said, " And have you no other weapons to fight with against spiritual wickedness as you call it? Search with the light of Christ in you and it will show you of whom you take counsel. . . . It is not my own life I seek, but the life of the seed which I know the Lord hath blessed. And I know this; that if you confirm your law, the Lord will overthrow both your law and you, by his righteous judgments and plagues poured justly upon you. In love and in the spirit of meekness, I again beseech you, for I have no enmity to the persons of any: but you shall know that God will not be mocked."

Viewed from a literary, moral, or religious standpoint, Mary Dyer's letters (and this is equally true of the letters and other writings of very many early Quakers) compare favorably with the best efforts of the leading Puritans. Daniel Gould, a comparatively illiterate Quaker, wrote a letter dated " rod Iland the 3 month 1660," and addressed "To the rulers & people of the town & jurisdiction of bostene." He appealed to them as follows: "I am grieved to see your cruelty and your hard-heartedness against a people that cannot flatter you nor willfully do you any wrong, but if any should do you any wrong or trespass against any man, let a righteous law take hold of such; but what need any law be made against the innocent, those that do you no wrong. . . . Concerning religion let every one be fully persuaded in his own mind and worship according as God shall persuade his own heart, and if any worship not God as they ought to do and yet liveth quietly and peaceably with their neighbors and countrymen and doeth them no wrong, is it not safer for you to let them alone to receive their reward from him who said, I will render vengeance to mine enemies and reward them that hate me. . . . Let God alone be Lord of the conscience, and not man, and let us have the same liberty and freedom amongst you, as other Englishmen have to come and visit our friends and kindred and do that which is honest and lawful to be done in buying or selling; and if any have a mind to reason or speak concerning the way and worship of God, that they may not be put in prison or punished for it, and so let people have liberty to try all things and hold fast that which is good."[1] Had the rulers heeded the advice of this uneducated but liberal and clear-headed Quaker, instead of the bigoted counsel of the cultivated and accomplished John Norton, they might have established a civil and religious order in the colony which would have forever marked them as just and enlightened legislators.

The second proposition to be considered is, that whereas Dr. Ellis's arraignment of Friends gives the impression that extravagant and offensive behavior was the rule with them, the truth is that their extravagances were comparatively infrequent, and, aside from their use of emphatic scriptural language, were exceptional.

The third statement is, that the persecution of Friends was not only not the result, but was the direct cause of such improprieties as may be proved upon them. These two propositions may be considered jointly.

As fair specimens of the invective indulged in by the Quakers, Dr. Ellis quotes

[1] For this and other Quaker letters, see Appendix, pp. 202-222.

some harsh language from the journal of Humphrey Norton, which he found in the British Museum. It is not in any of our libraries, but other Quaker works, written during the same period, confirm the belief that Friends, smarting under a sense of wrong and personal injury, did not hesitate to call men and things by their right names. And yet they were quick to forgive, and they bore no malice. Their denunciation of persecution and superstitious church ordinances was scriptural almost without exception. It is impossible for any one to cite a single instance of indecent railing by a Quaker, such as we have seen was indulged in with comparative impunity by the Puritan Edmund Batter, a government official and church-member. It may not only be admitted, but all lovers of fair play must find satisfaction in the fact, that Friends resorted to scriptural weapons in the unequal conflict. It is questionable, however, whether the practice was so habitual with them as is represented. It is more probable that their invective was the special utterance extorted by special or specific deeds of Puritan violence. The Puritan court records seem to confirm this view, for the reports of arrests and trials are remarkably free from charges of rudeness of either speech or behavior, and it is noteworthy that in the scriptural argument against Quakerism written by John Norton and published by order of the General Court, October 18, 1659, it is alleged that " the practice of the Quakers . . . is to belch out railing and cursing speeches," but the accusation is qualified by the words, " some of them at least." [1] It is a mistake to suppose that those Friends who indulged in what, to polite ears of this age, sounds extravagant and ill-mannered, were in any way peculiar, or that they spoke in an unknown tongue; for they merely conformed to the manners and customs characteristic of the age in which they lived, and especially characteristic of the Puritans. This has already been demonstrated as to England, in the preceding pages, by quotations from Puritan authors who called clergymen of the Established Church " Baalites and Balaamites," and the " service book " an " abomination," and by citations of the acts and language of other men and writers, including Milton. In New Eng-

[1] See Appendix, p. 147

land the same customs were prevalent. The Puritans were forward to abuse men with their tongue, and were perfectly at home in the vindictive vernacular. We have already observed how impossible it was for them to enact a law aimed at Friends, without ushering it in with a vituperative epithet. In these laws and other documents we are made familiar with such terms as cursed sect of hereticks, blasphemouth opinions, devilish opinions, pestilent errors and practices, diabolical doctrine, pernicious sect, horrid tenets, instrument of satan, rogues and vagabonds, incorrigible rogues, etc. Charles Chauncey, President of Harvard College, in urging the enforcement of capital punishment, spoke of six Quaker prisoners as "six wolves in a trap," to which, in a later day, Elizabeth Hooten retorted by denouncing the college as "a cage of unclean birds."

In Hutchinson's History it is related that at the ordination of Mr. Higginson, in 1660, John Smith of Salem was arrested for making a disturbance by crying out, "What you are going about to set up, our God is pulling down;" while Bishop, without, however, designating the time or occasion, quotes

Higginson as stigmatizing the Quaker's Inward Light as "a stinking vapor from hell." Were not the Puritans quite equal to the Friends in extravagance of language and the use of harsh and vindictive epithets?

It is commonly understood that the Quakers constantly interrupted the religious meetings and the famous Thursday lecture of the Puritans, but this is an error started by some malicious or careless commentator and greedily adopted by others. In rare instances, such as the one Hutchinson relates, they may have done so; but both Puritan and Quaker records prove that the Friends, as a rule, waited until service had ended, before delivering their testimony, and the same witnesses prove that instead of being impelled by an "aimless spirit of annoyance" to address church congregations, they were inspired by an enlightened distrust of religious ordinances and Christian ministration that fostered superstition, dogmatism, and persecution. When they attempted to hold their own meetings, they were violently assaulted, their houses were invaded, and they were haled before the magistrates. A very large number of the arrests, of which there is any report, were made because Friends refused to attend church and bravely maintained their right to hold meetings of their own. Edmund Batter, the two Archers, Benjamin Felton, Henry Skerry — all church-members — and Thomas Roots, are named by Bishop as the "bloody huntsmen" who made themselves especially prominent in ferreting out Quaker meetings and dragging the "cursed heretics" to judgment. The Quakers were persecuted and goaded into going to the sanctuary of these inquisitors, and, when meeting or lecture was over, protesting against such outrages and the wickedness of both Christian ministers and the religion that sanctioned them. A careful search shows that in two instances the Friends enforced their righteous protests by the unique method of breaking bottles. Two women, Sarah Gibbons and Dorothy Waugh, went through this dramatic performance in "2d Month, 1658," in the presence of John Norton, "as a sign of his emptiness." Both of them had been, previously, the victims of persecution. In 1663, Thomas Newhouse, another sufferer, bore his testimony in the same manner, crying out, "So they should be dashed in pieces." Newhouse subsequently fell from grace, and was disowned as an apostate by more sober Friends, to whom he was a frequent source of trouble.[1] When Wenlock Christison was on trial for his life, in 1661, Catherine Chattam attended court, appropriately clothed in sackcloth and ashes. It is reported, also, that Elizabeth Hooten,[2] who came here with an express permit from the King to purchase property and to become a resident, but was refused permission to do so by the authorities, was arrested as a "vagabond" and barbarously whipped for crying aloud, "Repent," in the streets of Cambridge. Old records and authorities contain these and a few other illustrations of what are known as the extravagances of the Quakers; but instead of bristling all over with them as Puritan apologists would have us believe, it is impossible to find any considerable number, and the few that are to be found are readily traced to the persecution. Some of the more familiar instances are counted as men in buckram by the excited imagina-

[1] William Edmundson's *Journal*, p. 69.
[2] Believed to be the first convert to Quakerism made by George Fox. See brief account of her sufferings in Appendix, p. 177.

tions of writers, who magnify their number to a degree that would honor Falstaff.

The most serious of all the charges on the score of extravagance deserves separate consideration. One has a right to infer from the sketch Dr. Ellis has given of the state of affairs during the period which he describes, that it was not uncommon for Quaker women to parade the streets and to enter the churches unattired, and that the colonial authorities were goaded into a resort to barbarous legislation by such wild and crazy freaks.[1] There is a serious misapprehension of the truth here. The records furnish instances of two women who were literally stripped of their clothing by the authorities; and many other instances of women who were stripped from the waist upwards and exposed to public gaze, but from the arrival of Mary Fisher and Ann Austin upon these inhospitable shores, in 1656, down to the passage of the "vagabond law" in May, 1661, in which the cruelties of corporal punishment culminated, — during this entire time, there was not a single case of such social indecorum by the Qua-

[1] *Massachusetts and its Early History;* also *The Memorial History of Boston.*

kers, — not one. Dr. Ellis cites the case of a woman who appeared in this condition in Boston, her body being smeared with black paint. He is wrong. The record shows that this woman, Margaret Brewster, was abundantly clothed, and it also shows that *this event occurred in the year* 1677 ;[1] *that is, fifteen years after the last year of the times of which Dr. Ellis professes to give a history!* In two instances only, once in " 9th mo. 1662" and once in May, 1663, women appeared in public without their garments, and in both cases their acts were the result of persecution. A detailed report of the Wardwell case may serve to help us in accounting for them. Thomas Wardwell was a Puritan and a freeman of the Massachusetts colony. He lived in Boston, where on November 23, 1634, his son Eliakim was baptized. Eliakim removed to Hampton about the year 1659. It is not known at what time he embraced the Quaker faith, but on April 8, 1662, he was fined for absence from church on twenty-six Sabbaths. In December, 1662, Ann Coleman, Mary

[1] Judge Sewall's *Diary*, vol. i. p. 43. For a very interesting report of Margaret Brewster's trial, etc., see Appendix, pp. 193–202.

Tomkins, and Alice Ambrose, at the instigation of Rev. Mr. Rayner, and by order of deputy magistrate Richard Walden, were stripped naked from the middle upward, tied to a cart, and, though the weather was "bitter cold," were driven through several towns. On arrival at each town they were cruelly whipped. At Dover, while the flogging was being administered, the Rev. Mr. Rayner " stood and looked and laughed at it," whereupon Eliakim Wardwell, who was also present, reproved the reverend gentleman for his brutality, and thereby added one more piece of insolence to the list of Quaker " outrages." For this offensive behavior he was put in the stocks along with William Fourbish, who had also manifested irreverence by rebuking the pious Rayner. Soon after this event, Wardwell harbored and entertained his friend Wenlock Christison. Such an offense was too grievous to be overlooked, and the Rev. Seaborn Cotton, with truncheon in hand, headed a party of order-loving citizens, and marched from his own home to the house of Wardwell, some two miles away. Christison received him and asked him " what he did with that club in his hand." Pastor Cotton replied, saying, " he came to keep the wolves from his sheep." Christison was immediately seized and dragged away. The wolf having been secured, Wardwell, who, as head of the family, was the bell-wether of Mr. Cotton's flock of sheep, was summoned to court and fined. To satisfy the fine, his saddle-horse was taken from him. The horse was worth fourteen pounds, and as this sum exceeded the fine, a vessel of green ginger was left at his house to settle the account. But the green ginger speedily went the way of the horse, for Wardwell was soon fined again for his own and his wife's absence from church, and in time was rendered almost penniless by repeated seizures of his property. The Rev. Seaborn Cotton, it seems, had a sharp eye for business, and, knowing the Wardwells would not pay for preaching they did not hear and would not countenance by their presence, he shrewdly sold his "rate" — the sum of money the Wardwells were obliged by law to contribute to his support — to one Nathaniel Boulter. How large a share this dealer in lapsed church tithes charged Cotton, we shall never know. We do know, however, that before he concluded the bargain he visited the

Wardwells under pretense of borrowing a little corn for himself, which they willingly lent him. Having thus surreptitiously discovered the quantity of corn in the crib, and its whereabouts, he, "Judas-like," went and bought the "rate" and then returned and "measured the corn away as he pleased."

Lydia Wardwell was married to Eliakim, October 17, 1659. She also was a Puritan, and a church-member to the manor born, being the daughter of Isaac Perkins, who was a freeman of the colony. She is described as "a young and tender, chaste woman," and was no doubt such. She became a Quaker, with her husband, and in a loyal, wifely way had shared the trials and sufferings to which they had been doomed during the few years of their married life. She knew the story of Ann Austin and Mary Fisher; she probably had witnessed the flogging of her own friends, Ann Coleman, Mary Tomkins, and Alice Ambrose, and had heard the laughter of the Christian minister, as the lash descended upon their naked bodies. Four of her friends had been hanged and scores of others tortured. The guest of her fireside had been kidnapped under her eyes; the rapacious church tithe dealer and pious magistrates had stripped her home of even the grass that grew in the meadow. The burden laid upon this bride was too heavy for her young spirit, and, in the light of a subsequent event, it is reasonable to suppose that it produced mental aberration. The original narrator of her sad experience states that while these troubles fell thick and fast and heavily upon her, she was repeatedly sent for, to go to church, "to give a reason" for her separation from it. Pestered and goaded by these demands, and probably with an imagination disordered by her sufferings, she answered a summons in May, 1663, by disrobing her body and, in this condition, entering the church. It was "exceeding hard," the narrator says, "to her modest and shamefaced disposition," to pass through this terrible ordeal. She went thus as a "sign" of the spiritual nakedness of her persecutors. This strange and dreadful scene occurred at the church in Newbury. The sequel is far more shocking to us than the deed itself. The poor soul was arrested and on the 5th of May, 1663, was sentenced by the court at Ipswich to "be severely whipped and pay costs and fees to the marshall of Hampton for bringing her, 10s. 6d. and fees, 2s. 6d." In accordance with this sentence " she was tied to the fence post of the tavern . . . stripped from her waist upwards, with her naked breasts to the splinters of the posts and then sorely lashed with twenty or thirty cruel stripes." [1] Previous to this, in 9th mo. of 1662, Deborah Wilson, who had passed through much the same scenes and sufferings, appeared, in the same manner and for the same purpose, in the streets of Salem. In her case the constable, Daniel Rumbal, it is said, took compassion on her, and she escaped with only moderate chastisement. It is quite possible that the constable had misgivings, or, it may be, positive information regarding her mental condition; for, subsequently and after persecution was measurably abated, she was arraigned " for frequently absenting herself from the public ordinances," and was dismissed because, as the court record reads, " she is distempered in her head."

The acts of Lydia Wardwell, Deborah Wilson, Thomas Newhouse, and Margaret Brewster play a conspicuous part in the

[1] *New England Judged*, pp. 376–377.

Quaker melodrama which we are told preceded the Puritan tragedy. The truth is, they were not the prelude but the afterpiece and the sequel to the tragedy. They are, however, repeatedly and persistently cited in order to justify or to extenuate the cruelties of the Puritan rulers. Such acts, we are told, might well drive a sober people to desperation, and tempt them to resort to the most severe remedies. But will some apologist take the trouble to explain by what process of reasoning the legislation of 1656 to 1661 can be attributed to offenses committed in 1662, 1663, and 1677? History must be read backwards that this intellectual feat may be performed.

The popular apologies for the Puritans, that now pass for history and are to be read in the pages of standard works (notably those of Palfrey and Bancroft), as well as in the historical essays of many other writers, are based upon an unwarrantable exaggeration of the character and number of Quaker offenses and upon a reckless confusion of dates.[1] This serious and fatal defect necessarily renders such historical crit-

[1] Bryant and Gay's *Popular History of the United States* is a notable exception.

icism not only worthless but pernicious. The modern Quaker has a right to appeal from the fiction to the truth of history in vindication of his ancestors. There are scholars in the old Bay State who are never backward when the Puritan fathers are to be defended. They are competent by knowledge, experience, and ability to investigate and to report. Let any one of them examine all the records carefully, with an eye for the truth, and publish the evidence upon which the verdict of these popular writers is supposed to rest. It will be found to be astonishingly meagre. Though "screaming out through barred windows" is believed to have been a popular Quaker method of bearing testimony, but few such cases are to be found, and they were justified by the provocation. Friends were sometimes punished by being put in the stocks, and occasionally, while enduring this enforced degradation, they testified aloud against the wickedness and cruelty of the authorities. Unless it can be shown that the prisoners were punished because of some social disorder, it would be unfair to class such acts as extravagances. Instances of the kind are very rare. If they are numerous, let us have them.

Interruption of church service occurred just often enough to suggest the popular fiction as to its frequency. Down to the passage of the inhuman law of May, 1661, the offenses were confined almost exclusively to righteous rebuke of persecution, sometimes by letter and sometimes verbally. Attempts to address the ministers and people at the close of sermon or lecture may have occurred a dozen times during the entire six years, though ordinary authorities do not furnish so many cases. Whether or not this class of offenses should be ranked with the " extravagances," can be determined better after the whole matter has been carefully reviewed. After the execution of four Quakers, and especially after the passage of the law of May, 1661, or, to put it in another way, as the persecution waxed hotter, the testimony of Friends became more marked, and perhaps more frequent, but even then the number of those who were guilty of improper acts was by no means great. When we remember the bitter and persistent provocation, we can but admire the calm, quiet, and dignified self-restraint exhibited by "most" of them. Should any competent Puritan apologist attempt the examination suggested, let us have in full the "wild rant," the outcome of "besotted stupidity," with the circumstances under which it was uttered, and the date. Let him cite every case of Quaker indecorum and indecency he can find, stating exactly what was done or said, and giving the precise, or, if it is not known, the approximate date of each event. Let him arrange these cases in the order of their occurrence, and, side by side with them, quote the Puritan laws with the dates of their passage, and, also, all other provocatory acts of the authorities. Let him report each in the proper order of time — the numerous arrests, the indictments, the pleas of the prisoners, the notes of the magistrates, the trials, convictions, sentences, and punishments inflicted, just as he finds them on the records. It will not suffice to say that, in general terms, the Puritans accused the Quakers of "contemptuous behavior to authority," unless substantiating evidence of the alleged misdemeanor is produced, for, as has already been shown, the Puritan officials did not hesitate to bear false witness concerning the victims of their pious wrath. Such evidence is clearly of slight value and inadmissible, unless it is competent for one and the same party to perform the functions of judge, jury, prosecuting attorney, and witness, all in one. It must be remembered, too, that by " contemptuous behavior " the magistrates often referred to the Quaker's custom of wearing the hat, to his use of the singular number in addressing one person only, and to his refusal to take the oath. These customs were not aimed at authority, nor were they subversive of social order, but, as the Puritans well knew, they were matters of conscience. It was, and is, manifestly absurd to pretend that while the Friends wore hats in their own assemblies and addressed each other in the plain language, they wore the same hats and used the same style of speech, in the presence of government officers and church ministers, as a mark of their contempt.

Too much of special pleading, reckless writing, and rhetoric, have been expended on this subject. It is time now for the presentation of an impartial statement of the truth, unadorned by efforts of the imagination. We need a well considered judgment based upon the plain facts. The tenor of such judgment is beyond question.

It will be found that "most" of the Massachusetts Quakers were not ignorant and lawless, nor seditious and pestering, nor rancorous and indecent, but that they were fully as intelligent and well-informed, often more enlightened, and, on the whole, quite as well behaved and as guiltless of social indecorum as the Puritans themselves.

A fair examination can result only in a complete overthrow of the theory that they were the aggressors, and "wantonly initiated the strife," and that by their wild misdeeds the Puritans were "beyond measure provoked and goaded to the course which they pursued." It will be seen that the Quakers, not the Puritans, were goaded and tormented, and that it is a reversal of the truth to put it otherwise. Another cause for Puritan cruelty must be discovered. We have yet to learn what Quaker offense so frenzied Bellingham as to drive him to inflict such barbarous treatment upon Ann Austin and Mary Fisher, immediately upon their arrival here, in the early part of 1656; what the outrage that "goaded" Governor Endicott into forwarding his letter from Salem, saying, had he been at home, he " would have had them well whipped"; what the nature of the offenses that led to the imprisonment and treatment as criminals of Christopher Holder, Thomas Thirstone, William Brend, John Copeland, Mary Prince, Sarah Gibbons, Mary Whitehead, Dorothy Waugh, and Richard Smith, when they first came here, in 1656. The list of objurgations and indecencies that, in October, 1656, " stung and goaded " the Puritans into passing the first act in the series of cruel legislation is yet to be given. The story of Nicholas Upsall should follow this recital. The checkered career of this brave old man will serve to indicate the " seditious and rancorous " character of the Quakers.

Mary Dyer and Anne Burden were the first Quaker visitors who arrived after the passage of the law of 1656. Mary Dyer's career, and especially her bearing when she faced death on Boston Common, will illustrate the " dogged pertinacity " with which she persecuted her reluctant executioners. Endicott, it is said, gave her an opportunity to save her life by lying, which, however, she was too obstinate to do. This pure, intelligent, and devoted woman is pilloried in history [1] as one " of the most insufferable

---

[1] *Memorial History of Boston*, vol. i. p. 168.

tormentors" of Boston. Of what insufferable acts was she guilty? What is the evidence upon which this description of her is based? The story of her companion is not so widely known. It is interesting as a bit of evidence to show how the authorities were made desperate by the intrusiveness of Quakers.

Anne Burden was not a preacher. She came here to settle the estate of her deceased husband. Bellingham, before whom she was arraigned, could find no fault in her, but said " she was a plain Quaker and must abide the law." Though ill at the time, she was thrust into gaol where she was detained about three months. During her imprisonment some tender-hearted people collected debts for her to the value of thirty pounds. Finally, she was shipped direct to England. Her request to be allowed to go to Barbadoes, as her goods would bring a better price there, was refused. Her property was assessed fourteen shillings to satisfy the gaoler's fee, and seven shillings for boat hire to carry her to the ship — for though the captain offered to carry her in his own skiff, without charge, she was compelled to go with the hangman, who, at her expense, had provided one. She was further robbed of goods to the value of six pounds ten shillings, for her passage, of which the captain never received a shilling. She, however, on reaching London, though under no obligation to do so, paid him in full. It is to be hoped that when the Puritan version of this "intrusive" Quaker's story is told, we shall learn what became of the six pounds ten shillings, of which she was distrained, though it may be that in the "frenzy" of the moment, produced by her "pestering and indecent" conduct, such trifles were overlooked. Let some one name, if he can, a single act of this woman or a single act of any one of the few Quakers who preceded her, that justifies or palliates the treatment she received.

Another class of Quaker intruders has its place in our early history. Their "lawless fanaticism," as indicated by the evidence about to be given, may help to explain how the magistrates were beyond endurance provoked by these aggressors and "wanton initiators" of strife. It appears that James Cudworth, a magistrate of New Plymouth and a captain, was left off the bench and lost his captaincy, because he had entertained some Quakers at his house in order to become better acquainted with their principles, which, however, he never adopted. He says, "the Quakers and I cannot close in divers things, and so I signified to the court I was no Quaker, . . . but as I was no Quaker, so I would be no persecutor." This Puritan Cudworth wrote a letter, dated in the 10th month, 1658, graphically describing the condition of affairs in both colonies, in which he says of the Quakers, "They have many meetings and many adherents; almost the whole town of Sandwich is adhering towards them. . . . The Sandwich men may not go to the Bay, lest they be taken up for Quakers; W. Newland was there about his occasions, some ten days since, and they put him in prison twenty-four hours, and sent for divers to witness against him, but they had not proof enough to make him a Quaker, which, if they had, he should have been whipped; nay, they may not go about their occasions in other towns of our colony, but warrants lie in ambush to apprehend and bring them before a magistrate to give an account of their business. Some of the Quakers in Rhode Island came to bring them goods, to trade with them, and that for far reasonabler terms than the professing and oppressing merchants of the country, but that will not be suffered." Referring to the imitation of the Massachusetts Bay magistrates by the Plymouth authorities, in their persecution of Quakers, he significantly says, " and now Plymouth-saddle is on the Bay horse." This remarkable letter[1] is too long for reproduction here, but any detailed recital of evidence would be incomplete without it. It is a curious commentary upon the " aimless spirit of annoyance " that led many of the " pestering and intrusive " Quaker visitors to the Bay. The letter is also of collateral value here, because it suggests the correction of a very serious error which occurs in an essay by Judge William Brigham, published by the Massachusetts Historical Society. Judge Brigham asserts, with evident satisfaction, that in New Plymouth colony there was a " law against Quaker Ranters, but no Quaker had a hair of his head hurt." Judicially speaking, it may be true that the Quaker hair was not pulled in Plymouth as it was in Boston, but Judge Brigham ought to have

[1] See Appendix, pp. 162–172.

known, and might easily have learned, that the Plymouth authorities, though less harsh and vindictive than their neighbors, were nevertheless adepts in the business of scourging Quakers. What are we to expect from untrained men, when a distinguished member of the bar is so heedless in his statements?

It is by no means necessary to produce the entire record in order to confirm the views expressed, or the positions taken here, in opposition to opinions and theories that prevail in the popular mind; but the Puritan apologist who cares to revise his judgment should read the whole of it. In his review of 1658 he will not overlook the glass bottle feat of Sarah Gibbons and Dorothy Waugh, but when he tires of this scene, let him leave the church and watch for a moment the threefold knotted whip as the lash descends upon the back of Hored Gardner. If he will listen closely, he will hear this Quaker woman's voice, as it ascends to Heaven, pleading for forgiveness of the persecutors.[1]

[1] See Appendix, pp. 172, 173.

CHAPTER V.

THE CAUSE OF THE WAR AND ITS RESULTS.

DR. ELLIS says " our Fathers cared little, if at all, for the Quaker theology. They did not get so far as that in dealing with them." On the contrary, their abhorrence of the religious opinions or belief of the Friends was the real cause of the persecution.

The cardinal principles and leading tenets of Quakerism have been detailed in a preceding chapter, and therefore only brief mention of them is necessary here. In common with the Puritans, Quakers believed in the doctrine of original sin, the Christian atonement, a future life either in heaven or hell, and the inspiration of the Bible. In common with the Puritans, they condemned as idolatrous the ceremonial service of the Established Church, but they also denied the efficacy of ordination, baptism, formal prayer, and the sacrament of the Lord's supper. They sought to restore the spirituality and simplicity of primitive Christianity. Their reliance upon what they called the Inward Light, as a sufficient guide in matters of religion, has always distinguished them from all other religious sects. This Inward Light may be briefly explained as follows: God is an indwelling Spirit, and Humanity is His holy temple. His law is written upon the hearts of all men, and obedience to it will lead them into all truth, so far as religious truths are revealed to men. Through the operation of this law the soul of man is accessible to his Creator. It is the rule of life to which every one must subject himself, and out of which duty is evolved.

The Quakers were further distinguished from other sects by their determined championship of religious freedom. With other men religious liberty was a matter of opinion and political policy, but in the Quaker philosophy it stood as a divine principle and an inalienable birthright.

New England Puritans denounced the Quaker Light as an *ignis fatuus*, and a "stinking vapor from hell." For spiritual and moral guidance they relied solely upon the revealed law as contained within the limits of the Bible, and especially the Old Testament, and, we might add, they rested their ecclesiastical, civil, and penal legislation upon the same authority. They attempted to build up a theocratic government. Leaving their native homes to escape persecution, they established themselves here, only to deny religious liberty to all comers. Toleration was only second to heresy in their list of pernicious errors. If we fully realize the differences that separated them from the Quakers, we shall see that a conflict between the two was inevitable. Resistance to religious tyranny was an imperative and sacred duty with the Quaker. Extermination of heresy and persecution of non-conformists were essential articles in the creed of the Puritans. Let us review the evidence.

The first reference to Quakers in the colonial records speaks of their "abounding errors." The first two Quakers arrive and are found to hold " very dangerous heretical and blasphemous opinions." They are closely confined until they can be sent away in order " to prevent the spread of their corrupt opinions." The first count in the indictment embodied in the preamble of the first law aimed at Quakers is stated in the emphatic words, "cursed heretics," and, as has been shown, succeeding laws are aflame with charges of heresy and blasphemy. In October, 1658, John Norton was employed by the Court to write an exposure and refutation of Quaker errors. The order reads, "Whereas this Court, well understanding the dangerous events of the doctrines and practices of the Quakers, hath by law endeavored to prevent the same, but finding that some of them do dispense their papers, so expressing themselves therein as that they may deceive divers of weak capacities, and so draw them in to favor their opinions and ways, — now, for the further prevention of infection, and guiding of people in the truth, in reference to such opinions, heresies, or blasphemies by them expressed in their books, letters, or by words openly held forth by some of them, the Court judgeth meet that there be a writing or declaration drawn up, and forthwith printed," etc. In November, 1659, the Court, "by the honored Governor," thanked Mr. Norton " for his great pains and worthy labors in the tractate he drew up, and by order of this Court hath been printed, wherein the dangerous errors of the Quakers is fully refuted and discovered, and to acquaint him that this Court hath given him five hundred acres of land . . . as a small recompense for his pains therein."

When this same Christian minister, John Norton, volunteered to defend the inhuman gaoler who treated William Brend with such horrible barbarity, it was not because Brend was guilty of any breach of the civil law, but because " he endeavored to beat our Gospel ordinances black and blue." In October, 1658, a petition addressed to the Court, asking for additional legislation against the Quakers, complains of " their denial of the Trinity, . . . of the person of Christ, . . . of the Scriptures as a rule of life." [1] In December, 1660, in an address sent by the General Court to King Charles II., the Quakers were complained of as " open and capital blasphemers, open seducers from the glorious Trinity, the soul's Christ, our Lord Jesus, the blessed gospel, and from the Holy Scriptures as the rule of life," etc.

In the file of unpublished manuscript in the state-house, Boston, there are papers

[1] See Appendix, p. 154.

indexed, " Minutes of the Magistrates," dated 1659-60, and headed, "The Examination of Quakers at ye Court of Assistants in Boston."[1] These papers do not indicate the specific charges upon which the Quakers were arrested, but are evidently memoranda made during the progress of the trials. In this collection there are forty entries. Three of them are too brief and indefinite to indicate their subjects; three state that some of the prisoners entered court with their hats on; one states that two of them disturbed the court and were carried out by the gaoler; one refers to a statement made by some one else, that there was a woman at Salem, " Consader Southwick," who said she was greater than Moses, for she had seen God oftener than he had. (This was, no doubt, a slander.) Of the others, six mention the protests of the prisoners against the " wicked law," and *twenty-six* refer to the religious opinions expressed by, and, it is presumable, drawn from them in the process of examination.

In view of this evidence and other facts heretofore narrated, one is forced to the conclusion that our fathers were not only not

[1] See Appendix, pp. 157-161.

indifferent to the theology, or what they called the heresy, of the Quakers, but that the policy of persecution which they inaugurated immediately upon the advent of the despised and hated sect is directly chargeable to their detestation of the alleged heresy, and to their fear of its baleful influence upon the colony. It is no exaggeration to assert that the Quakers were dealt with almost exclusively on the score of their religious opinions.

It has been said that a realization of the radical differences between the Friends and Puritans will lead to the conclusion that the conflict was inevitable, but to appreciate fully the nature of that conflict, it is important to understand their agreements. The coming of the Quakers into Massachusetts, as the subject is popularly treated, suggests the descent of a horde of semi-barbarians with pagan customs, grotesque manners, and lawless habits, upon a God-fearing, sober, and law-abiding community. This misconception is fatal to a proper understanding of our early history. Quakerism, historically defined, was an outgrowth of Puritanism. Its ranks were recruited from the English yeomanry. Some of the Friends, before their conversion to peace principles, had served in the armies of Cromwell, and most of them had been attached to one or the other of the non-conformist or Puritan churches. This is especially true of the New England Quakers. They were Englishmen by birth and blood, and Puritan by education. While adopting the distinctive principles of Quakerism, they retained the characteristics that distinguished the Puritan from the Cavalier. The martyrs, Robinson, Stevenson, and Leddra, who, by the decree of Endicott, Bellingham, and Norton, were hanged on Boston Common, rivaled their executioners in their hostility to the Established Church and in their virtuous horror of the profligacy and licentiousness of the English court. The Quaker testimonies, as enumerated in the Book of Discipline, find their counterpart in the sumptuary laws that grace the statute book of the Massachusetts colony.[1] The two

---

[1] Referring to these laws and to the prevailing dress of the colonists, Mr. H. E. Scudder well says that "the Puritans . . . vainly sought for a correspondence between the outer man and the inner sanctified spirit." This is equally true of the Quakers, but the same writer classifies them as a people "who wished to strip off all obstructions to the exhibition of Nature." It would be useless to attempt to characterize such

parties held in common a living faith in the wisdom and power of simplicity, sobriety, and godliness, combined with more or less enlightened theories of religious and social equality and intellectual liberty. The interpretation of the moral law by either party was equally destructive to social sin, and equally conducive to social welfare. All Puritans were not Quakers, but all Quakers were Puritans. Strong sympathies and similarities intensified the heat of the conflict. Family feuds are proverbially bitter, and theirs was a family quarrel. When Greek met Greek, then came the tug of war. Fortunately the methods of warfare were radically different. The one resorted to coercion and the tortures of the Inquisition to enforce an iron will, while the other relied solely upon passive but inflexible resistance, patient endurance, aggressive argument, exhortation, and appeals to conscience.

It is often urged that the Puritan rulers frequently " disclaimed power over the faith and consciences of others," [1] and that their

writing. It is easier to believe it was a slip of the pen, and, if so, one that both Mr. Scudder and the editor of the *Memorial History of Boston* will always regret. See vol. i. p. 484.

[1] *Massachusetts and its Early History*, p. 437.

futile effort to keep the Quakers from entering or residing in the colony was only a defense against the "confusion and anarchy" that would surely follow if they were tolerated here. This apology is as untenable as the others which have been examined. A disclaimer, to be of value, must be sustained by corresponding action, and the founders abundantly disproved the sincerity of these professions. Their treatment of adherents to the Established Church of England may be in part accounted for by the fear of the establishment of Episcopacy here as a political power, under the auspices of the English government, but there is no such excuse for their treatment of Baptists and Quakers. They were resolved, at all hazards, to control the faith and consciences of the whole colony. We have seen that they were unremitting in their efforts "to prevent the spread of corrupt opinions." Quaker books were prohibited, men were disfranchised for harboring Friends, Quaker meetings were assaulted and dispersed, and could be attended only at the risk of fine and imprisonment. Non-attendance at the regular church on the "Lord's day" was a criminal offense. The county court records show that at Ipswich and Salem alone, during the four years from 1658 to 1661 inclusive, there were one hundred and thirty-eight convictions for attending Quaker meetings and absence from public worship. As there were but two hundred and eight Sabbaths in the four years, the number of convictions seems sufficiently great, but, had there been a separate conviction for each offense, it would be very much greater. The officials would allow their victims to live unmolested for several consecutive weeks, and would then swoop down upon them. The following entries illustrate their methods.

County Court, Salem, 20th 5mo 1658. — " Provided Sothwick convicted of her being frequently absent from publike worship on the Lord's day & alsoe is sensured to pay 20^s for being present at two meetings of Quakers and alsoe is to be sett by the feet in the stockes one hower for chargeing the court to be persecutors — to pay 5^s costs court."

" Nicholas Phelps is sensured by this court to pay 40^s to the treasurer of this county for defending a quakers meeting & allsoe to be sent to the house of correction at Ipswich for owning himselfe to be a quaker & there to continue this Courts pleasure: to pay costs 30ˢ."

"30 : 9ᵐᵒ. 1658. The wife of George Gardner is fined by this Court 40ˢ for 8 dayes absence from yᵉ publique worship of God, the Lord's daies."

The iron rule of conformity was nowhere more savagely enforced than in Massachusetts. When at last Quaker fidelity to the cause of religious liberty overcame the almost indomitable will of the rulers and achieved a lasting triumph over despotic bigotry, toleration succeeded persecution with beneficent results. All dread, real or pretended, of violence and disorder, vanished, and the Quakers were recognized as law-abiding citizens, upright, intelligent, peaceable, and useful members of society.

We are constantly reminded that in order to judge the policy and acts of the Puritans fairly we must remember that the colony was settled during the first half of the seventeenth, and not the last half of the nineteenth century. Only superficial criticism will apply the tests of our present civilization to events that occurred two hundred and twenty years ago. That which would be condemned in Boston to-day might have been applauded in Boston in 1660. These suggestions are pertinent, but are they not equally so when the Quakers are called to judgment? Let the persecutor and his victim stand or fall by the same rules of historical criticism. One representative writer[1] draws a pleasant picture of the peaceable, refined, and genial Quaker whom one may meet at any time in our streets and public assemblies, and to whom the epithet "sly" is the harshest that can be applied. This exemplary citizen, he assures the reader, is a very different person from the Quaker with whom the Puritans had to deal. This ingenious appeal would be more just had it been supplemented by the further reminder that the liberal, courteous, and progressive descendants from Puritan stock seen in our business marts, court-rooms, and pulpits, and to whom the epithet "smart Yankee" is the most severe we can apply, is a very different man from the Puritan with whom the early Quakers dealt. The contrast between Elizabeth Hooten and Lucretia Mott is far less marked than the contrast between Edmund Batter and Nathaniel Very,

[1] Dr. Ellis.

the present treasurer of the town of Salem. Our Buffums, Shattucks, and Southwicks are not exact copies of their Quaker ancestors who bore these names, and we shall all agree that our well-known Endicotts, Nortons, and Higginsons are a vast improvement upon their Puritan forefathers.

The age of Puritanism was an age of religious bigotry, intolerance, and persecution, relieved, however, by the liberal teaching of Milton and many other enlightened men of genius and talent. In New England, Rhode Island was the silver lining to the dark cloud that overhung Massachusetts. The liberal principles and policy of Williams, Arnold, and the Quakers, Coddington and Easton, put to shame the rulers of this colony. The average New England Puritan was far behind contemporary English reformers, but the rulers here were behind the average New England Puritan. This was partly due to the system of government by which all citizens except church-members were disfranchised. The magistrates and ministers were reactionists, and were not sustained even by their own followers. Their mission here, accepting their own statement as to what it was, met with a richly deserved fate. It was almost a complete failure. Their plan of government was repudiated and was succeeded by wiser political arrangements and more humane laws. Their religion, though it long retained its hold in theory, was displaced by one less bigoted and superstitious. It is now a thing of the past, a mere tradition, an antiquated curiosity.

The early Quakers, or some of them, in common with the Puritans, may illustrate some of the least attractive characteristics of their time; but they were abreast, if not in advance, of the foremost advocates of religious and civil freedom. They were more than advocates; they were the pioneers who by their heroic fortitude, patient suffering, and persistent devotion rescued the old Bay colony from the jaws of the certain death to which the narrow and mistaken policy of the bigoted and sometimes insincere founders had doomed it. They forced them to abandon pretentious claims, to admit strangers without insulting them, to tolerate religious differences, and to incorporate into their legislation the spirit of liberty which is now the life-blood of our institutions. The religion of the society of Friends is still an active force, having its full share of influence upon our civilization. The vital principle — "The Inward Light" — scoffed at and denounced by the Puritans as a delirium, is recognized as a profound spiritual truth by sages and philosophers.

APPENDIX.

COLONIAL LAWS FOR THE SUPPRESSION OF QUAKERS. MASS. RECORDS, VOL. IV.

Att a Generall Co᠁t, held at Boston 14, of October, 1656.

WHEREAS there is a cursed sect of hæreticks lately risen vp in the world, wch are comonly called Quakers, who take vppon them to be imediately sent of God and infallibly asisted by the spirit to speake & write blasphemouth opinions, despising gouernment & the order of God in church & comonwealth, speaking evill of dignitjes, reproaching and revjling magistrates and ministers, seeking to turne the people from the faith, & gajne proseljtes to theire pernicious wajes, this Court, taking into serious consideration the p'mises, and to prevent the like mischiefe as by theire meanes is wrought in our native land, doth hereby order, and by the authoritje of this Court be it ordered and enacted, that what master or comander of any ship, barke, pinnace, catch, or of any other vessell that shall henceforth bring into any harbor, creeke, or coue wthin this jurisdiccōn any knoune Quaker or Quakers, or any other blasphemous hæreticks, as aforesajd, shall pay, or cawse to be pajd, the fine of one hundred pounds to the Tresurer of the countrje, except it appeare that he wanted true knowledg or information of theire being such; and in that case he hath libertje to cleare himself by his oath when sufficijent proofe to the contrary is wanting, and for default of payment, or good securitje for it, shall be comitted to prison, & there to contjnew till the sajd sōme be sattisfied to the Tresurer as aforesajd; and the comander of any such ship or vessell that shall bring them (being legally convicted) shall giue in sufficijent securitje to the Goûno^r, or any one or more of the magistrates who haue power to determine the same, to carry them backe to the place whence he brought them; and, on his refusall so to doe, the Gouerno^r, or one or more of the magistrates, are hereby impowered to issue out his or theire warrants to comitt such master or comander to prison, there to continew till he shall give in sufficijent securitje to the content of the Gouerno^r or any of the magistrates as aforesajd. And it is hereby further ordered & enacted, that what Quaker soeuer shall arive in this countrje from forraigne parts, or come into this jurisdiccõn from any parts adjacent, shall be forthwith comitted to the house of correction, and at theire entrance to be seuerely whipt, and by the master thereof to be kept constantly to worke, & none suffered to converse or speak wth them during the tjme of

APPENDIX. 135

theire imprisonment, wch shall be no longer than necessitje requireth. And further, it is ordered, if any pson shall knowingly import into any harbor of this jurisdiccon any Quakers bookes or writings concerning theire diuilish opinions, shall pay for euery such booke or writting, being legally prooued against him or them, the some of five pounds ; and whosoeuer shall disperse or conceale any such booke or writing, and it be found wth him or her, or in his or her howse, and shall not imediately deliuer in the same to the next magistrate, shall forfeite and pay five pounds for the dispersing or concealeing of euery such booke or writing.

And it is hereby further enacted, that if any person wthin this colonje shall take vppon them to defend the hæretticall opinions of the sajd Quakers, or any of theire bookes or papers as aforesajd, ex annimo, if legally prooved, shall be fined for the first tjme forty shillings ; if they shall persist in the same and shall so againe defend it, the second tjme fower pounds ; if still, notwthstanding, they shall againe so defend & maintajne the sajd Quakers hæretticall opinions, they shall be comitted to the howse of correction till there be convenjent passage for them to be sent out of the land, being sentenced by the Court of Asistants to banishment. Lastly it is heereby ordered, that what pson or persons soeuer shall revile the office or pson of magistrates or ministers, as is usuall with the Quakers, such person or psons shall be seuerely whipt, or pay the some of five pounds. This order was publised 21: 8 m°, 56, in seuerall places of Boston, by beate of drumme.

Att a Gennerall Court, held at Boston, 14 of October, 1657.

As an addition to ye late order in reference to the coming or bringing in any of the cursed sect of the Quakers into this jurisdiction, it is ordered, that whosoeuer shall from henceforth bring or cawse to be brought, directly or indirectly, any knoune Quaker or Quakers, or other blasphemous hæreticks, into this jurisdiccōn, euery such person shall forfeite the some of one hundred pounds to ye countrje, and shall by warrant from any magistrate be comitted to prison there to remajne till the pœnalty be sattisfjed and pajd; and if any person or persons wthin this jurisdiccōn shall henceforth entertajne and conceale any such Quaker or Quakers or other blasphemous hæreticks, (knowing them so to be) euery such person shall forfeite to the countrye forty shillings for euery howers entertajnment and concealement of any Quaker or Quakers, as aforesajd, and shall be comitted to prison, as aforesajd, till the forfeitures be fully sattisfied and pajd.

And it is further ordered, that if any Quaker or Quakers shall presume, after they haue once suffered what the lawe requireth, to come into this jurisdiccōn, euery such male Quaker shall for the first offenc haue one of his eares cutt

APPENDIX.

off, and b kept at worke in the howse of correction till he cann be sent away at his oune charge, and for the second offenc shall haue his other eare cutt of, &c. and kept at the howse of correction, as aforesaid; and euery woman Quaker that hath suffered the lawe heere that shall presume to come into this jurisdiccōn shall be severely whipt, and kept at the howse of correction at worke till she be sent away at hir oune charge, and so also for hir coming againe she shall be alike vsed as aforesajd; and for euery Quaker, he or she, that shall a third tjme heerein againe offend, they shall haue theire toungues bored through wth a hot iron, & kept at the howse of correction, close to worke, til they be sent away at theire oune charge. And it is further ordered, that all & euery Quaker arising from amongst ourselves shall be dealt wth & suffer the like punishment as the lawe provides against forreigne Quakers.

At a Gennerall Courte held at Boston, the 19th of May, 1658.

That Quakers and such accursed hæreticques arising amongst ourselves may be dealt withall according to theire deserts, and that theire pestilent errors and practizes may speedily be prevented, itt is heereby ordered, as an addition to the former lawe against Quakers, that euery such person or persons professing any of their pernitious wajes, by speaking, writting, or by meetings on the Lords day, or any other tjme, to strengthen themselves or seduce others to theire djabolljcall doctrine, shall, after due meanes of conviction incurre the pœnalty ensuing; that is, euery person so meeting shall pay to the countrje for euery tjme tenn shillings, and euery one speaking in such meetings shall pay five pounds a peece, and in case any such person hath binn punished by scourging or whipping the first tjme, according to the former lawes, shall be still kept at worke in the house of correction till they put in securitje wth two sufficjent men that they shall not any more vent theire hatefull errors, nor vse theire sinfull practizes, or els shall depart this jurisdictjon at theire oune charges; and if any of them returne againe, then each such person shall incurre the pœnalty of the lawes formerly made for straingers.

Att the second Sessions of the Generall Court, held at Boston, the 19*th of October,* 1658.

Whereas there is a pernitious sect, comonly called Quakers, lately risen, who, by word & writing, haue published & maintayned many dajngerous & horrid tennetts, and doe take vpon them to chainge and alter the received laudable customes of our nation in giving ciuill respect to æqualls or reuerence to superiors, whose actions tend to vndermine the authority of civill gouernment, as also to destroy the order of the churches, by denying all established formes of worship, and by wthdrawing from the orderly church assembljes allowed & approoved by all orthodox proffessors of the truth, and insteed thereof, and in opposition therevnto, frequenting private meetings of theire oune, insinuating themselves into the minds of the simpler, or such as are lesse affected to the order & gouernment in church and comonwealth, whereby dieuerse of our inhabitants haue binn infected & seduced, and notw^{th}standing all former lawes made (vpon experience of theire arrogant, bold obtrusions to disseminate theire principles amongst vs) prohibbitting theire coming into this jurisdiction, they haue not binn deterred from theire impetuous attempts to vndermine our peace and hasten our ruine.

For prevention whereof, this Court doth order and enact, that euery person or persons of the cursed sect of the Quakers, who is not an inhabitant off but found w^{th}in this jurisdiction, shall be app'hended (without warrant), where no magistrate is at hand, by any connstable, comissioner, or selectman, and conveyed from connstable to connstable, vntill they come before the next magistrate, who shall comitt the sajd person or persons to close prison, there to remajne with out bayle vntill the next Court of Asistants, where they shall haue a legall trjall by a speciall jury, & being convicted to be of the sect of the Quakers, shall be sentenced to bannishment, vpon pajne of death; and that euery inhabitant of this jurisdiction being convicted to be of the aforesajd sect, either by taking vp, publishing, & defending the horrid opinions of the Quakers, or by stirring vp mutiny, sedition, or rebelljon against the government, or by taking vp theire absurd and destructiue practises, vizt, denying civil respect & reuerence to æqualls & superiors, wthdrawing from our church assembljes, & insteed thereof frequenting private meetings of their oune in opposition to church order, or by adhering to or approoving of any knoune Quaker, or the tenetts & practises of the Quakers, that are opposite to the orthodoxe received opinions & practises of the godly, and endeavoring to disaffect others to ciuill gouernment & church order, and condemning the practise & proceedings of this Court against the Quakers, manifesting thereby theire compljance wth those whose designe it is to ouerthrow the order established in church and comonwealth, euery such person, vpon examination & legall conviction before the Court of Asistants, in manner as aboue sajd, shall be comitted to close prison for one moneth, and then, vnlesse they choose voluntarily to depart the jurisdiction, shall giue bond for theire good abbearance & appearance at the next Court of Asistants, where continuing obstinate and refusing to retract & reforme the aforesajd opinions and practises, shall be sentenced to bannishment upon pajne of death; and in case of the aforesajd voluntary departure, not to remajne or againe to returne into this jurisdiction wthout the alowance of the majo^r part of the councill first had & published, on pœnalty of being banished vpon pajne of death; and any one magistrate, vpon information giuen him of any such person, shall cause them to be app'hended, and if, vpon examination of the case, he shall, according to his best discretion, finde just ground for such complainte, he shall comitt such person to prison vntill he come to his trjall, as is aboue expressed.

Att a Generall Court of Election, held at Boston, 22d May, 1661.

This Court, being desirous to try all meanes, wth as much lenity as may consist wth our safety, to prevent the intrusions of the Quakers, who, besides theire absurd & blasphemous doctrine, doe, like rouges & vagabonds, come in vpon vs, & haue not bin restreined by the lawes already provided, haue ordered, that euery such vagabond Quaker found wthin any part of this jurisdiction shall be app'hended by any person or persons, or by the connstable of the toune wherein he or she is taken, & by the connstable, or, in his absence, by any other person or persons, conveyed before the next magistrate of that sheire wherein they are taken, or comissioner invested wth magistratticall power, & being by the sajd magistrate or magistrates, comissioner or comissioners, adjudged to be a wandering Quaker, vizt, one that hath not any dwelling or orderly allowance as an inhabitant of this jurisdiction, & not giving ciuil respect by the vsuall gestures thereof, or by any other way or meanes manifesting himself to be a Quaker, shall, by warrant vnder the hand of the sajd magistrate or magistrates, comissioner or comissioners, directed to the connstable of the toune wherein he or she is taken, or in absence of the connstable, or any othere meete person, be stripped naked from the midle vpwards, and tjed to a carts tayle, & whipped thro^h the toune, & from thence imediately conveyed to the connstable of the next toune, towards the borders of our jurisdiction, as theire warrant shall direct, & so from connstable to connstable till they be conveyed thro^h any the outward most tounes of our jurisdiction. And if such vagabond Quaker shall returne againe, then to be in like manner app'hended & conveyed as often as they shall be found wthin the limitts of our jurisdiction, provided euery such wandering Quaker, hauing beene thrice convicted & sent away as abouesajd, & returning againe into this jurisdiction, shall be app'hended & comitted by any magistrate or comissioner as abouesajd vnto the house of correction wthin that county wherein he or shee is found untill the next Court of that County, where, if the Court judge not meete to release them, they shall be branded with the letter R on theire left shoulder, & be severely whipt & sent away in manner as before ; and if after this he or shee shall returne againe, then to be proceeded against as incorrigible rogues & ennemys to the comon peace, and shall imediately be app'hended & comitted to the comon jayle of the country, and at the next

APPENDIX. 143

Court of Asistants shall be brought to theire tryall, & proceeded ag^t according to the lawe made anno 1658, page 36, for theire banishment on payne of death. And for such Quakers as shall arise from amongst ourselves, they shall be proceeded ag^t as the former lawe of anno 1658, page 36, doth provide, vntill they haue beene convicted by a Court of Asistants; & being so convicted, he or shee shall then be bannished this jurisdiction; & if after that they shall be found in any part of this jurisdiction, then he or shee so sentenced to banishment shall be proceeded against as those that are straingers & vagabond Quakers in manner as is aboue expressed. And it is further ordered, that whatsoeuer charge shall arize about app'hending, whipping, conveying, or otherwise, about the Quakers, to be layd out by the connstables of such tounes where it is expended, & to be repajd by the Tresurer out of the next country levy; and further, that the connstables of the seuerall tounes are hereby empowred from tjme to tjme, as necessity shall require, to impresse cart, oxen, & other asistance for the execution of this order.

The following Scriptural argument, "To vindicate the justice of this Courts proceedings in refference to the Quakers," was circulated throughout the Mass. Colony, by order of the "Generall Court" Oct. 18th, 1659:

APPENDIX.

Many of that sect of people which are comonly called Quakers hauing, from forreine parts & from other colonjes, come at soundry times and in seuerall companjes & noumbers into this jurisdiction of the Massachusetts, & those lesser punishments of the house of corrections & imprisonment for a tjme hauing beene inflicted on some of them, but not sufficing to deterr & keepe them away, but that still they haue presumed to come hither, vpon no other ground or occasion (for ought that could appeare) but to scatter theire corrupt opinions, & to drawe others to theire way, & so to make disturbance, and the honnored Generall Court having herevpon made an order & lawe, that such persons should be bannished & remooved hence, on pajne of death, to be inflicted on such of them, as after theire bannishment should presume to returne & come hither againe, the making & execution of the aforesajd lawe may be cleered to be warrantable & just vpon such grounds & considerations as these, viz.:

1. The doctrine of this sect of people is destructive to fundamentall trueths of religion, as the sacred Trinitje, the person of Christ & the holy Scriptures, as a perfect rule of faith & life, as Mr Norton hath shewed in his tractate against the Quakers; yea, that one opinion of theires, of being perfectly pure and wthout sinne, tends to ouerthrow the whole gospell & the very vitalls of Christianitje, for they that haue no sinne, haue no neede of Christ, or of his sattis-

APPENDIX. 145

faction, or his blood to cleanse them from theire sinne; no need of faith to believe in Christ, for imputed righteousnes to justify them, as being perfectly just in themselves; no neede of repentance, as being righteous & wthout sinne, for repentance is only for such as have sinne; no neede of growing in grace, nor of the word and ordinances of God, that they may grow thereby, for what neede they to grow better who are already perfect? no neede of Christian watchfulnes against sinne who haue no such ennemy as sinne dwelling in them, as Paul had, but are free from the presence and being of sinne, & therefore Christ needs not to say to them, as sometjmes to his disciples, 'Watch & pray, that yee enter not into temptation; the spirit is willing but the flesh is weake'; for hauing no such flesh or weakenesse in them, they haue no such neede of watchfulnesse; they haue no neede to purify themselves dayly, as all Christians should, for they are perfectly pure already; no neede to put off the old man and put on the new, like the Christians to whom Paul wrote his Epistles, for what neede they to doe this when they are already wthout sinne, and so wthout all remainders of the old man? Such fundamentalls of Christianitje are ouerthroune by this one opinion of theires, & how much more by all theire other doctrines! Now, the comandment of God is plajne, that he that presumes to speake lyes in the name of the Lord & turne people out of the way which the Lord hath comanded to walk in, such an one must not liue, but be put to death; Zach. 13: 3; Deut. 13: 6; & 18: 20; & if the doctrine of the Quakers be not such, let the wise judge.

2. It is the comandment of the blessed God, that Christians should obey magistrates, Tit. 3: 1; & that euery soule should be subject to the higher powers, Rom. 13: 1; yea, be subject to euery ordinance of man for the Lords sake, 1 Peet. 2: 13; & yeeld honnor & reuerence or feare to such as are in authoritje, Prou. 24: 21; 1 Pet. 2: 17; & forbeare all cursing and reviling & evill speeches touching such persons, Exod. 22: 28; Eclesiast. 10: 20; Tit. 3: 2; Acts 23: 5; & accordingly good men haue beene wont to behaue themselves wth gestures and speeches of reuerence and honnor towards superiors in place and power, as Abraham bowed downe himself to the Hittites, Gene. 23: 7, 12; Jacob & his wives & children unto Esau, Gene. 33: 3, 6, 7; Josephs brethren vnto Joseph, being governor in Ægipt, Gene. 42: 6; & 43: 26 & 28; Joseph to his father Jacob, Gene. 48: 12; Moses to his father in lawe Jethro, Exod. 18: 7; Ruth to Boaz, Ruth 2: 10; Dauid to Saul, 1 Sam. 24: 6; . . . 1 Kings 1: 16, 23, 31; wth otherr that might be added. And for reviling or contemptuous speeches, they haue binn so farre therefrom that they haue spoken to and of theire superiors wth termes & expressions of much honor & reuerence, as father, 1 Sam. 19: 3; 1 Kings 19: 20; & 2: 2, 12; master, 2 Kings

APPENDIX.

6 : 15 ; 1 Sam. 24 : 6 ; lord, Gen. 33 : 13, 14 ; 1 Pet. 3 : 6 ; my lord, 1 Sam. 24 : 8 ; Gen. 44 : 18, 19, 20 ; 1 Sam. 1 : 15, 26 ; most noble Festus, Acts 26 : 25 ; most excellent Theophilus, Luke 1 : 3 ; and the like ; that servant of Abraham's, Gen. 24, doth call Abraham by the terme & title of master, a matter of twenty times or not much lesse, in that one chapter ; and on the contrary, it is noted as a brand & reproach of false teachers, that they despise dominion and are not afrajd to speake evill of dignitjes, 2 Pet. 2 : 10 ; Jude 8 ; though the very aingells would not doe so vnto the divill, 2 Peet. 2 : 11 ; Jude 9. Now, it is well knoune that the practize of the Quakers is but too like these false teachers whom the apostles speake of, & that they are farre from giving that honnor & reuerence to magistrates which the Lord requireth, & good men haue giuen to them, but on the contrary show contempt against them in theire very outward gestures & behavior, & (some of them at least) spare not to belch out rajling & cursing speeches. Wittnes that odjous, cursing letter of Humphrey Norton ; and if so, if Abishaj may be judge, they are worthy to die ; for so he thought of Shimej for his contemptuous carriage and cursing speeches against Dauid, 2 Sam. 16 : 9 ; & 19 : 21. And though Dauid at that tjme did forbeare to put him to death, yet he giues chardge to Solomon, that this Shimej hauing cursed him wth such a grievous curse, he should not hold him guiltlesse, but bring doune his

hoarje head to the graue wth blood, 1 Kings 2:
8, 9 ; according to which direction King Solomon
caused him to be put to death, Vers. 44, 46.

3. Also, in this story of Solomon & Shimej, 1
Kings 2, it is recorded how Solomon confined
Shimei to Jerusalem, chardging him vpon pajne
of death, not to goe out thence, & telling him
that if he did he should dye for it, which confinement when Shimej had broken, though it
were three yeares after, & vpon an occasion that
might seeme to haue some weight in it, viz., to
fetch againe his servants that were runne away
from him, yett for all this, the confinement being
broken, Solomon would not spare him, but putts
him to death ; and if execution of death be lawfull for breach of confinement, may not the same
be sajd for breach of bannishment? Confinement, of the two, may seeme to be much
sleighter, because in this a man is ljmited to one
place & debarred from all others, whereas in
bannishment a man is debarred from no place
but one, all others being left to his liberty ; the
one debarres him from all places, saue that it
giues liberty to one ; the other giues liberty to
all places, saue that it restraines from one ; and
therefore if death may be justly inflicted vpon
breach of confinement, much more for returne
vpon bannishment, which is these Quakers case.

4. There is no man that is possessed of house
or land, wherein he hath just title & propriety as
his oune, but he would count it vnreasonably
injurious that another who had no authoritje

thereto should intrude & enter into his house wthout his, the ouno^{rs} consent; yea, and when the ouno^r doth expressly prohibitt & forbidd the same. Wee say, when the man that so presumes to enter hath no authoritje thereto; for if it were a connstable or other officer legally authorized, such an one might indeed enter, notwthstanding the householders dissent or charge to the contrary; but for them that haue no authoritje the case is otherwise. And if such one should presume to enter into another man's house & habitation, he might justly be impleaded as a theife or an vsurper; & if in case of such violent assault, the owno^r should, *se defendendo,* slay the assaylant & intruder, his blood would be vpon his oune head. And if private persons may in case shed the blood of such intruders, may not the like be graunted to them that are the publicke keepers and guardians of the comonwealth? Haue not they as much power to take away the liues of such, as contrary to prohibition, shall jnvade & intrude into theire publicke possessions or territorjes as private and particcular persons to deale so wth them that, wthout authoritje, shall presume to enter into theire private & particcular habitations? which seemes clearly to be the present case; for who cann belieue that Quakers are connstables ouer this colonje, to intrude themselves, invade, & enter, whither the colonje will or no, yea, & notwthstanding theire expresse prohibition to the contrary? If in such violent and bold attempt they loose theire liues, they may thank themselues as the blameable cause & autho^{rs} of theire oune death.

5. Who cann make question but that a man that hath children & family both justly may, & in duty ought to, preserue them of his chardge (as farre as he is able) from the daingerous company of persons infected wth the plague of pestilence or other contagious, noysome, and mortall diseases? and if such persons shall offer to intrude into the mans house amongst his children & seruants, notwthstanding his prohibition and warning to the contrary, & thereby shall jndainger the health & liues of them of the familje, cann any man doubt but that in such case the father of the familje, in defence of himself & his, may wthstand the intrusion of such infected & daingerous persons & if otherwise he cann not keepe them out, may kill them? Now, in Scripture, corruption in minde & judgment is counted a great infection & defilement, yea, & one of the greatest; for the apostle, saying of some men that to them there is nothing pure, giues this as the reason of it, because euen theire minde & conscience is defiled, Tit. 1 : 15; as if defilement of the minde did argue the defilement of all, & that in such case there was nothing pure; euen as when leprosie was in the head, the preist must pronounce such a man vtterly vncleane, sith the plague was in his head, Levitt 13 : 44. And it is the Lords comand that such corrupt persons be not re-

APPENDIX. 151

ceaved into house, 2 John 10, which plainly enough impljes that the householder hath power to keepe them out, & y^t it was not in theire power to come in if they pleased, whither the householder would or no. And if the father of a particcular family may thus defend his children & household, may not magistrates doe the like for theire subjects, they being nursing fathers and nursing mothers by the account of God in Holy Scripture? Isaj. 49 : 23d. Is it not cleare, y^t if the father in the family must keepe them out off his house, the father in the comonwealth must keepe them out of his jurisdiction? And if sheepe & lambes cannot be preserved from the dainger of woolves, but the woolves will breake in amongst them, it is easy to see what the shephard or keeper of the sheepe may lawfully doe in such a case.

6. Itt was the comandment of the Lord Jesus Christ vnto his disciples, that when they were persecuted in one citty, they should flee into another, Math. 10 : 23 ; & accordingly it was his oune practise so to doe many a tjme, both when he was a child, Math. 13 : 14 ; & afterwards, 12 : 15 ; Joh. 7 : 1 & 8 ; last, 10 : 39 ; and so was also the practise of the saints.

Wittnes what is written of Jacob, Gen. 27 : 42, 43 & 28 : 5 ; of Moses, Exod. 2 : 14, 15 ; of Eljas, 1 Kings 19 : 3 ; of Paul, Acts 9 : 24, 25, 29, 30, & 17 : 13, 14 ; & of the apostle, Acts 14 : 4, 5, & others, who when they haue beene persecuted, haue fled away for theire oune safety; and reason requires that when men haue liberty vnto it, they should not refuse so to doe, because otherwise they will be guilty of tempting God, & of incurring theire oune hurt, as having a faire way open for the avoyding thereof, but they needelessly expose themselves thereto. If therefore, that which is donne against Quakers in this jurisdiction were indeed persecution, as they account of it, (though in trueth it is not so, but the due ministration of justice; but suppose it were as they thinke it to be) what spirit may they be thought to be acted & led by, who are in theire actings so contrary to the comandment & example of Christ & of his saints in the case of persecusion, which these men suppose to be theire case? Plaine enough it is, that if theire case were the same, theire actings are not the same, but quite contrary, so that Christ and his saints were led by one spirit, and those people by another; for rather then they would not show theire contempt of authoritje, and make disturbance amongst his people, they choose to goe contrary to the expresse directions of Jesus Christ, & the aprooved examples of his saints, although it be to the hazard & perrill of theire oune liues.

PETITION FOR SEVERER LAWS AGAINST THE QUAKERS, OCTOBER, 1658.[1]

To the Honored General Court now afsembled at Boston.

THE humble Petition of vs whose Names are Vnderwritten: Humbly sheweth.

That where as through the good hand of the Lord, this Country hath for seuerall yeares past, by means of the pious care & faithfullnes of those which haue satt att ye helme, beene preserued from many menacing dangers, both as to its ciuill & religious interest, in respect of wch we may not but allwayes acknowledg o^rselues wth great thankfullnes debtors to the Lord first, and then to o^r gouernors in the Lord yett finding by experience, Satan is not wanting to this day by himself and instrum^{ts} to attempt new wayes, vnto the disturbing, nay we may truly say the Subverting of o^r ciuill & religious Polities, as well as in other p^{r}ts.

And although, this hath in its measure beene taken notice of, & foreseene by this Hon^d Court in respect of many who haue of late audaciously intruded themselues among vs, vnder the name of Quakers, whence your pious Endeauours haue beene exerted to free vs of soe great an Euill threatned.

Notwithstanding, in so much as the prouision

---

[1] Massachusetts Archives, vol. x. p. 246.

y^t is already made [by reason of their prodigious insolency] doth not secure vs of the future enjoym^t of o^r ciuill & religious Libertyes, as is to be desired. Wee therefore take o^{r}selues bound, both in conscience to God, and faithfullnes to this Gouermn^t and people, whereof we are a part, to present the following Propositions to yor most serious considerations, & y^t at such a time.

1st. Not here to examine their malignity ags^t the establishm^t of ciuill Gouermn^t, in the hands of any such, as is subseruient to ye end thereof vizt the good of ye people.

whether these persons, are not indeed to be looked at, as professed Enemies to ye christian Magistrate,[1] and open Seducers of ye people therefrom, where they are permitted to be, they calling disobedience, vnto a great part of ye 5th Commandm^{tt}, obedience : we say of ye 5th commandm^t, ye foundatiō of ye p^{r}cepts of ye 2^d table, and this they hauld forth as openly, if not as much, as ags^t ye power of ye Magistrate, in matters of religion belonging to the first Table.

2^{ly}. Whether, their practise vnder pretence of new light, tends not manifestly, to ye vtter subversion of the verry body of religion, witnes, their deniall of the Trinity, y^t is to say, the Trinity of persons, or distinct subsistances in ye diuine nature, their deniall of ye person of Christ, of ye Scripturs as a rule of life, & of ye whole church jnstitution of ye Gospell, ye ordinary means appointed for ye conuersion and edification of Soules.

[1] See Capital Law title Conspiracy.

APPENDIX. 155

3^(ly). Whether, their incorrigiblenes after soe much means vsed both for their conviction, & preserving this place from contagion, being such, as by reason of their malignant obduratices, dayly increaseth rather then abateth o^r feare of ye Spirit of Muncer, or Jo^n of Leyden reviued, & consequently of some destructiue euill impending : Itt be not necessary, after ye example of other christian comon weales infected wth pests, not more perillous then these are, and ye common & vniuersally approued argum^t of *se defendendo*, vpon ye sad experience of ye remedy hitherto applyed, is not only not effectuall, but contemned, and abused wth ye highest hand, if after ye sentance of banishm^t added therevnto, they shall still presumptuously obtrude themselues vpon this jurisdiction, wheth^r we say, it be not necefsary to punish soe high incorrigiblenes, in such and soe many capitall euills, wth death, rather y^n expose religion, this gouermn^t, & ye whole people to both temporall and etern^ll ruine. And as for any y^t may arise among o^rSelues after conviction of being quakers wth an admonition therevnto, they shall still continue obstinate, y^r then they in like man^r may be sentenced to banishm^t, and if thay shall againe presumptiously obtrude themselues vpon this jurisdiction, y^t y^en thay may be proceeded wth as ye others.

Much Hon^d these Propositions humbly & religiously presented [yor Servants are far frō prescribing any thing to yor wisdomes] wth o^r prayers y^t a diuine Sentence may proceed out of yor mouth, & y^t yor lips may not transgress in judgm^t, concerning some effectuall & speedy expedient, y^t may crowne you with being ye jnstrumentall Sauior^s of this people, in soe weighty a cause, & in this hower of N E temptation and together wth deliuerance from o^r feares, minister matter of perpetuall thanksgiuing on yor behalfe vnto o^rselues, who are

Yo^{rs} most humbly devoted in all christian Service.

Wm Dauis	Natha: Duncan
James Johnson	John Wilson
Nathaniell Williams	Will Colbron
Henry Powning	James Penn
John Euered alies Webb	Ed Raynsford
Hezekiah Vsher	Robert Waker
Thomas Bumsted	Tho Marshall
Tho Clark	Will Hudson
Theodore Atkinson	William Salter
Willyam Dinsdale	Henry Phillips
Tho: Snow	Thomas Savage
John Hull	John Newgate
Anthony Stoddard	

THE EXAM. OF QUAKERS AT Y^E COURT OF ASSISTANTS IN BOSTON, MARCH 7, '59-60.[1]

Joseph Nicholson, Jane his wife, and Wainslocke Christophersonne.

Christopher sayth he owns ye Scripture to be a true declaracon of X^t & be true words; he saith ye mind of God man must know as they did wch gave forth ye Scriptures; X^t is ye rule for evrie one to walk by.

X^t is ye word.

the letter kills; ye Spirit giveth life.

I have not put ye Scripture in ye roome of X^t.

Nichols to ye Govr: thou errest, not knowing ye Scripture nor ye pow^r of God, thou art not come to y^t wch gave forth ye Scriptures. God heareth us, all th. is but jangling.

Christ. X^t sayth sweare not at all, love y^r enemies, & *he* y^t swears is out of ye Doctrine of X^t.

Nicholson. you er from ye Scripture in keeping ye 1st day instead of ye Sabbath. Wee owne ministers of ye word, but not of ye letter. they y^t take titles were nev^r sent of God.

that X^t in whom I believe is a Spirit. a savio^r to ye M^ajor Denis: thou nev heardest by voice. hearken to ye voyce of X^t w^thin.

: y^t will shew the thy sins.

Christoph. he hath a body. one body, & one spiritt. & no other but w^t is meant in y^t place Preaching. reading. singing. done by y^t

---

[1] Massachusetts Archives, vol. x. pp. 261-264.

Spirit of yᵉ Lord we owne. All other is an abominacon.

Christoph. in obedience to yᵉ Lord we come hither.

Nicholson. Wee owne quakering to be of God, and wee owne quakers whom you so call to be children of God & to be of yᵐ they call quakers.

Christopher & Jane also answered Each of yᵐ for thems. that they were of them they called Quakers.

The Jury was called over to yᵐ all, and libty given to yᵐ all to challenge any of yᵐ off yᵉ Bench.

March 8ᵗʰ, 1660.

Joseph Nicholson sayth yᵉ law agˢᵗ Quakers is a wicked law, & not of God.

His wife denyes yᵉ law as not of God.

W. Christophson sayth as a witness for God & his law he stands agˢᵗ you & yoʳ law, & yᵗ yᵉ law agˢᵗ yᵉ quakers is agˢᵗ yᵉ law of God and is a corrupt law neither pure nor holy, seeking for bloud; & Christ fulfilled yᵉ law wᶜʰ appoint murderers to be put to death.

Sayth he saw yᵉ law before he came at M, & he came for a testimony agˢᵗ this cruelty ; & the God of order yᵉ know not. In yᵉ name & feare of God I am come.

J. N. sayth yᵉ God yᵗ *made Heaven & Earth* is not yoʳ God.

W. C. sayth the true God yᵗ made heaven & earth we *know & owne*.

APPENDIX. 159

Math. Stanly sayth she bears witnes agst ye law, for X^t came not to kill but to save.

Wm. King sayth he is warned of God not to goe, & y^t he will stay, tho banished.

W. Christoph. sayth that he owned ye scripture to be a true declaraccon, but not ye mind of God, & sayth that we know not ye word of God, & y^t not one man here can prove ye scripture to be ye word of God. Sayth they are ye words of God, but not ye word; he sayth w^t he sayth is truth according to Scripture, & y^t he stands here a witnes for God.

Margarett Smith sayth she denies ye law, & stands as a *witnes* agst ye same.

Benj. Bulflower sayeth he hath fulfilled ye law of God, & *done* all y^t it reqiires.

Nich. Jno Endecutt. I stand as an evidence agst ye thou knowest not ye pow^r of God, & y^t wch thou callest heresie in me shall stand for ev. higher than thee, although as high as ye Pope.

Chambline. sayth y^t he find not ye opinion of ye Quakers to be cursed, but y^t wch shall stand when all yo^{rs} shall fall.

Wm King sayth he own ye Scripture to be a true declaraccon of ye word of God.

Mary Trask. & Smith & Martha Stanly. in a contemptuous & seditious mann. began & continued to speak. to ye disturbance of Court. so y^t ye Court was forced to charge ye Jailor to *cary y^m* out of ye Court.

Wm King sayth I am sure God doth & will *plead o^r cause.*

APPENDIX.

from Redding.

Benj. Bulflower came into Court wth his hat cockt: remaineing on his head. & refusing to pull it of w comanded. & said he could justifie his accon by ye Scripture. Alleading for his prooffe y^t Scripture. y^t God threatned his people y^t for y^r sin he would bring a nation agst y^m y^t would not Hon^r ye person of ye old man.

being examined in Court,

Asserted. y^t after ye Dissoluccon of ye Body & soule. ye body should nev be united to ye soule more. y^t ye first day of ye weeke was not ye sabboath but ye last day of ye weeke. ye 7th day.

Martha Stanly. late of tenterdon in Kent. & a single woman.

Saith she had a message from ye Lord. to vissitt her freinds in prison at Boston. her message was to turn people from darknes to light to ye virtues wthin: in her measure she hath spoaken ye same. & shall go on to ye laying down her life.

Saith wee meet wth many y^t tell us we must sin whiles we live.

as any keep to ye light made manifest in conscience they sin not.

Sayth I acknowledge my selfs to be one of y^m whom ye world in scorne call quakers.

Jno Chambline of Boston came into Court wth his Hatt on.

---

ffrom Salem.

Wm King wth his Hatt on & Mary Trask & Mary Smith came into Court.

owned y^t they were at a meeting at Whartons on ye Sabboath day. & y^t they were such as ye world called Quakers. this all of y^m pticularly owned.

Wm King sayth Wharton was not at home w they were there — and I am sure We have obeyed ye voyce of God in w^t we have done & God sayth wo. be to y^m pastors y^t destroy ye flock of X^t.

March 9, 60.

Major Hawthorne at Dinn^r wth ye Govr & maiestrates at a court of assistants, said that at Salem y^r was a woman called Consader Southîeck, y^t said shee was greater y^n Moses, for Moses had seen God but twice & his backe parts, & shee had seen him 3 times face to face, instancing the place (i. e.) her old House one time, & by such a swamp another time.

Also he said a woman of Lin being at y^t meeting w Wm Robinson was y^r who pressed much ye seeking for ye pow^r w^{t}hin. shee asked him How shee should come to feele ye pow^r wthin. He told her y^t shee must cast of all attendance to ordinances, as publike p^{r}ching, pray^r, reading ye Scripture, & attending to times of Gods wor^p, and then wayte for the communicaccon of ye pow^r wthn.

and He added y^t Hee y^t will do so, it will not be long, but ye Devill will appeare, either more explicitely, or at least implicitely to comunecate hims —

JAMES CUDWORTH'S LETTER, WRITTEN IN THE TENTH MONTH, 1658.[1]

As for the State and Condition of Things amongst us, it is Sad, and like so to continue; the Antichristian Persecuting Spirit is very active, and that in the Powers of this World: He that will not Whip and Lash, Persecute and Punish Men that Differ in Matters of Religion, must not sit on the Bench, nor sustain any Office in the Common-wealth. Last Election, Mr. Hatherly, and my Self, left off the Bench, and my self Discharged of my Captainship, because I had entertained some of the Quakers at my House, (thereby that I might be the better acquainted with their Principles) I thought it better so to do, than with the blind World, to Censure, Condemn, Rail at, and Revile them, when they neither saw their Persons, nor knew any of their Principles: But the Quakers and my self cannot close in divers Things; and so I signified to the Court, I was no Quaker, but must bear my Testimony against sundry Things that they held, as I had Occasion and Opportunity: But withal, I told them, That as I was no Quaker, so I would be no Persecutor. This Spirit did Work those two Years that I was of the Magistracy; during which time I was on sundry Occasions forced to Declare my Dissent, in sundry Actings of that Nature; which, altho' done with all Moderation of Expression, together with due respect unto

[1] *New England Judged*, p. 168.

APPENDIX. 163

the Rest, yet it wrought great Disaffection and Prejudice in them, against me; so that if I should say, some of themselves set others on Work to frame a Petition against me, that so they might have a seeming Ground from others (tho' first moved and acted by themselves, to lay me what they could under Reproach) I should do no Wrong. The Petition was with Nineteen Hands; it will be too long to make Rehearsal: It wrought such a Disturbance in our Town, and in our Military Company, that when the Act of Court was read in the Head of the Company, had not I been present, and made a Speech to them, I fear there had been such Actings as would have been of a sad Consequence. The Court was again followed with another Petition of Fifty Four Hands, and the Court return'd the Petitioners an Answer with much plausibleness of Speech, carrying with it great shew of Respect to them, readily acknowledging, with the Petitioners, my Parts and Gifts, and how useful I had been in my Place; Professing they had nothing at all against me, only in that Thing of giving Entertainment to the Quakers; whereas I broke no Law in giving them a Nights Lodging or two, and some Victuals: For, our Law then was, — If any Entertain a Quaker, and keep him after he is warned by a Magistrate to Depart, the Party so entertaining, shall pay Twenty Shillings a Week, for Entertaining them. — Since hath been made a Law, — If any Entertain a Quaker, if but a quarter of an Hour, he is to forfeit Five

Pounds. — Another, — That if any see a Quaker, he is bound, if he live Six Miles or more from the Constable, yet he must presently go and give Notice to the Constable, or else is subject to the Censure of the Court (which may be Hanging) — Another, — That if the Constable know, or hear of any Quaker in his Precincts, he is presently to apprehend him; and if he will not presently Depart the Town, the Constable is to Whip him, and send him away. — And divers have been Whipp'd with us in our Patent; and truly, to tell you plainly, that the Whipping of them with that Cruelty, as some have been Whipp'd, and their Patience under it, hath sometimes been the Occasion of gaining more Adherence to them, than if they had suffered them openly to have preached a Sermon.

Also another Law, — That if there be a Quaker Meeting any where in this Colony, the Party in whose House, or on whose Ground it is, is to pay Forty Shillings; the Preaching Quaker Forty Shillings; every Hearer Forty Shillings: Yea, and if they have Meetings, tho' nothing be spoken, when they so meet, which they say, so it falls out sometimes — Our last Law, — That now they are to be apprehended, and carried before a Magistrate, and by him committed to be kept close Prisoners, until they will promise to depart, and never come again; and will also pay their Fees — (which I perceive they will do neither the one nor the other) and they must be kept only with the Counties Allowance, which is but small (namely, Course Bread and Water.) No Friend may bring them anything; none may be permitted to speak with them; Nay, if they have Money of their own, they may not make use of that to relieve themselves. —

In the Massachusets (namely, Boston Colony) after they have Whipp'd them, and cut their Ears, they have now, at last, gone the furthest step they can: They Banish them upon pain of Death, if ever they come there again. We expect that we must do the like; we must Dance after their Pipe: Now Plimouth-Saddle is on the Bay-Horse (viz, Boston) we shall follow them on the Career: For, it is well if in some there be not a Desire to be their Apes and Imitators in all their Proceedings in things of this Nature. All these Carnal and Antichristian Ways being not of God's Appointment, effect nothing as to the Obstructing or Hindring of them in their Way or Course. It is only the Word and Spirit of the Lord that is able to Convince Gainsayers: They are the Mighty Weapons of a Christian's Warfare, by which Great and Mighty Things are done and accomplished. They have many Meetings, and many Adherents, almost the whole Town of Sandwich is adhering towards them; and, give me leave a little to acquaint you with their Sufferings, which is Grievous unto, and Saddens the Hearts of most of the Precious Saints of God; It lies down and rises up with them, and they cannot put it out of their Minds, to fee and hear of poor Families deprived of their Comforts, and brought into Penury and Want (you may say, By what Means? And, to what End?) As far as I am able to judge of the End, It is to force them from their Homes and lawful Habitations, and to drive them out of their Coasts. The Massachusets hath Banish'd Six of their Inhabitants, to be gone upon pain of Death; and I wish that Blood be not shed: But our poor People are pillaged and plundered of their Goods; and haply, when they have no more to satisfie their unsatiable Desire, at last may be forced to flee, and glad they have their Lives for a Prey.

As for the Means by which they are impoverished; These in the first place were Scrupulous of an Oath; why then we must put in Force an Old Law, — That all must take the Oath of Fidelity. — This being tendered, they will not take it; and then we must add more Force to the Law; and that is, — If any Man refuse, or neglect to take it by such a time, he shall pay Five Pounds, or depart the Colony. — When the time is come, they are the same as they were; Then goes out the Marshal, and fetcheth away their Cows and other Cattle. Well, another Court comes, They are required to take the Oath again, — They cannot — Then Five Pounds more: On this Account Thirty Five Head of Cattle, as I have been credibly informed, hath been by the Authority of our Court taken from them the latter part of this Summer; and these People say, — If they have more right to them, than themselves, Let them

APPENDIX.

take them. — Some that had a Cow only, some Two Cows, some Three Cows, and many small Children in their Families, to whom, in Summer time, a Cow or Two was the greatest Outward Comfort they had for their Subsistance. A poor Weaver that hath Seven or Eight small Children (I know not which) he himself Lame in his Body, had but Two Cows, and both taken from him, The Marshal asked him, What he would do? He must have his Cows. The Man said, — That God that gave him them, he doubted not, but would still provide for him. — To fill up the Measure yet more full, tho' to the further emptying of Sandwich-Men of their outward Comforts. The last Court of Assistants, the first Tuesday of this Instant, the Court was pleased to determine Fines on Sandwich-Men for Meetings, — sometimes on First Days of the Week, sometimes on other Days, as they say: They meet ordinarily twice in a Week, besides the Lord's Day, — One Hundred and Fifty Pounds, whereof W. Newland is Twenty Four Pounds, for himself and his Wife, at Ten Shillings a Meeting. W. Allen Forty Six Pounds, some affirm it Forty Nine Pounds. The poor Weaver afore spoken of, Twenty Pounds. Brother Cook told me, one of the Brethren at Barnstable certified him, That he was in the Weaver's House, when cruel Barloe (Sandwich Marshal) came to demand the Sum, and said, he was fully informed of all the poor Man had, and thought, if all lay together, it was not worth Ten

Pounds. What will be the End of such Courses and Practices, the Lord only knows. I heartily and earnestly pray, that these, and such like Courses, neither raise up among us, or bring in upon us, either the Sword, or any devouring Calamity, as a just Avenger of the Lord's Quarrel, for Acts of Injustice and Oppression; and that we may every one find out the Plague of his own Heart; and putting away the Evil of his own Doings, and meet the Lord by Entreaties of Peace, before it be too late, and there be no Remedy. Our Civil Powers are so exercised in Things appertaining to the Kingdom of Christ, in Matters of Religion and Conscience, that we can have no time to effect anything that tends to the Promotion of the Civil Weal, or the Prosperity of the Place; but now we must have a State-Religion, such as the Powers of the World will allow, and no other: A State-Ministry, and a State way of Maintenance: And we must Worship and Serve the Lord Jesus as the World shall appoint us: We must all go to the publick Place of Meeting, in the Parish where he dwells, or be presented; I am Informed of Three or Fourscore last Court presented, for not coming to publick Meetings; and let me tell you how they brought this about: You may remember a Law once made, call'd Thomas Hinckley's Law, — That if any neglected the Worship of God, in the Place where he lives, and sets up a Worship contrary to God, and the Allowance of this Government, to the publick Prophanation of God's

APPENDIX. 169

Holy Day and Ordinance, shall pay Ten Shillings, — This Law would not reach what then was aimed at: Because he must do so and so; that is, all things therein expressed, or else break not the Law. In March last a Court of Deputies was called, and some Acts touching Quakers were made; and then they contrived to make this Law serviceable to them; and that was by putting out the Word [and] and putting in the Word [or] which is a Disjunctive, and makes every Branch to become a Law. So now, if any do neglect, or will not come to the publick Meetings, Ten Shillings for every Defect. Certainly we either have less Wit, or more money, than the Massachusets: For, for Five Shillings a Day a Man may stay away, till it come to Twelve or Thirteen Pounds, if he had it but to pay them. And these Men altering this Law now in March, yet left it Dated, June 6. 1651. and so it stands as the Act of a General Court; they to be the Authors of it Seven Years before it was in being; and so you yourselves have your part and share in it, if the Recorder lye not. But what may be the Reason that they should not by another Law, made and dated by that Court, as well effect what was intended, as by altering a Word, and so the whole Sense of the Law; and leave this their Act by the Date of it charged on another Court's Account? Surely the Chief Instruments in the Business, being privy to an Act of Parliament for Liberty, should too openly have acted repugnant to a Law of England; but if they can do the Thing, and leave it on a Court, as making it Six Years before the Act of Parliament, there can be no danger in this. And that they were privy to the Act of Parliament for Liberty, to be then in being, is evident, That the Deputies might be free to act it. They told us, That now the Protector stood not engaged to the Articles for Liberty, for the Parliament had now taken the Power into their own Hands, and had given the Protector a new Oath, Only in General, to maintain the Protestant Religion; and so produced the Oath in a Paper, in Writing; whereas the Act of Parliament and the Oath, are both in one Book, in Print: So that they who were privy to the one, could not be Ignorant of the other. But still all is well, if we can but keep the People Ignorant of their Liberties and Priviledges, then we have Liberty to Act in our own Wills what we please.

We are wrapped up in a Labyrinth of Confused Laws, that the Freemens Power is quite gone; and it was said, last June Court, by one, — That they knew nothing the Freemen had there to do. Sandwich-Men may not go to the Bay, lest they be taken up for Quakers: W. Newland was there about his Occasions some Ten Days since, and they put him in Prison Twenty Four Hours, and sent for divers to Witness against him; but they had not Proof enough to make him a Quaker, which if they had, he should have been Whipp'd: Nay, they may not go about

APPENDIX.

their Occasions in other Towns in our Colony, but Warrants lie in Ambush to Apprehend and bring them before a Magistrate, to give an Account of their Business. Some of the Quakers in Rhode-Island came to bring them Goods, to Trade with them, and that for far Reasonabler Terms, than the Professing and Oppressing Merchants of the Country; but that will not be suffered: So that unless the Lord step in, to their Help and Assistance, in some way beyond Man's Conceiving, their Case is sad, and to be pitied: and truly it moves Bowels of Compassion in all sorts, except those in place, who carry it with a high Hand towards them. Through Mercy we have yet among us worthy Mr. Dunstar, whom the Lord hath made boldly to bear Testimony against the Spirit of Persecution.

Our Bench now is, Tho. Prince, Governour; Mr. Collier, Capt. Willet, Capt. Winslow, Mr. Alden, Lieut. Southworth, W. Bradford, Tho. Hinckley. Mr. Collier last June would not sit on the Bench, if I sate there; and now will not sit the next Year, unless he may have Thirty Pounds sit by him. Our Court and Deputies last June made Capt. Winslow a Major. Surely we are all Mercenary Soldiers, that must have a Major imposed upon us. Doubtless the next Court they may choose us a Governour and Assistants also. A Freeman shall need to do nothing but bear such Burdens as are laid upon him. Mr. Alden hath deceived the Expectations of many, and indeed lost the Affections of such, as

I judge were his Cordial Christian Friends; who is very active in such Ways, as I pray God may not be Charged on him, to be Oppressions of a High Nature.

THE STORY OF HORED GARDNER.[1]

Hored Gardner, who being the Mother of many Children, and an Inhabitant of Newport in Rhode-Island, came with her Babe sucking at her Breast, from thence to Weymouth (a Town in your Colony) where having finished what she had to do, and her Testimony from the Lord, unto which the Witness of God answered in the People, she was hurried by the baser sort to Boston, before your Governour, John Endicot, who after he had entertained her with much abusive Language, and the Girl that came with her, to help bear her Child, he committed them both to Prison, and Ordered them to be whipp'd with Ten Lashes a-piece, which was cruelly laid on their Naked Bodies, with a three-fold-knotted-Whip of Cords, and then were continued for the space of Fourteen Days longer in Prison, from their Friends, who could not Visit them. The Women came a very sore Journey, and (according to Man) hardly accomplishable, through a Wilderness of above Sixty Miles, between Rhode-Island and Boston; and being kept up, after your Cruel Usage of their Bodies, might have died; but you had no Consideration of this, or of them, tho' the Mother had of you, who after

[1] Reported in *New England Judged*, pp. 60, 61.

APPENDIX. 173

the Savage, Inhumane and Bloody Execution on her, of your Cruelty aforesaid, kneeled down, and Prayed — The Lord to Forgive you — which so reached upon a Woman that stood by, and wrought upon her, that she gave Glory to God, and said, — That surely she could not have done that thing, if it had not been by the Spirit of the Lord, — 11th of 3d Month, 1658.

RECAPITULATION OF THE SUFFERINGS OF LAURENCE AND CASSANDRA SOUTHICK.[1]

First, while members of their Church, they were both imprisoned for entertaining strangers, Christopher Holder and John Copeland, a Christian duty, which the apostle to the Hebrews advises not to be unmindful of. And after seven weeks imprisonment, Cassandra was fined 40s. for owning a paper written by the aforesaid persons. Next for absenting from the public worship and owning the Quakers' doctrine. On the information of one captain Hawthorn, they with their son Josiah were sent to the house of correction, and whipped in the coldest season of the year, and at the same time Hawthorn issued his warrant to distrain their goods for absence from their public worship, whereby there were taken from them cattle to the value of 4*l*. 15*s*. Again they were imprisoned with others for being at a meeting, and Cassandra was again whipped and upon their joint letter to the magis-

[1] Gough's *History of the Quakers*, vol. i. pp. 379-381.

trates before recited the other appellants were released, but this family, although they with the rest had suffered the penalty of their cruel law fully, were arbitrarily detained in prison to their great loss and damage, being in the season of the year when their affairs most immediately demanded their attendance. While they were in prison, William Maston coming through Salem in his way to Boston, brought them some provisions from home, for which he was committed to prison, and kept there fourteen days in the cold winter season, though about seventy years of age. And last of all were banished upon pain of death by a law made while they were imprisoned, and consequently against which they had not offended: Thus spoiled of their property, deprived of their liberty, driven into banishment, and in jeopardy of their lives, for no other crime than meeting apart, and dissenting from the established worship, the sufferings of this inoffensive aged couple ended only with their lives.

But the multiplied injuries of this harmless pair were not sufficient to gratify that thirst of vengeance which stimulated these persecutors, while any member of the family remained unmolested: During their detention in prison, they left at home a son and daughter named Daniel and Provided; these children, not deterred by the unchristian treatment of their parents and brother, felt themselves rather encouraged to follow their steps, and relinquish the assemblies of a people whose religion was productive of such

APPENDIX. 175

relentless persecution, for their absence from which they were fined 10*l.* though it was well known they had no estate, their parents having been reduced to poverty by repeated fines and extravagant distraints; wherefore to satisfy the fine, they were ordered to be sold for bond-slaves by the following mandate:" —

Att a Generall Court of Election, held at Boston, 11th of May, 1659.[1]

COUNTY TREASURER AUTHORIZED TO SELL QUAKERS.

Whereas Daniell and Provided Southwicke, sonne & daughter to Lawrence Southwicke, haue binn fyned by the County Courts at Salem & Ipswich, ptending they haue no estates, resolving not to worke, and others likewise haue binn fyned, & more like to be fyned, for siding wth the Quakers & absenting themselves from the publicke ordinances, — in ans^r to a quœstion, what course shall be taken for the sattisfaction of the fines, the Court, on pervsall of the lawe, title Arrests, resolve, that the Tresurers of the seuerall countjes are and shall hereby be impowred to sell the sajd persons to any of the English nation at Virginia or Barbadoes.

Letter of Laurence Southick and others.[2]

This to the Magistrates at the Court in Salem. Friends,

Whereas it was your pleasures to commit us

[1] *Mass. Records*, vol. iv. p. 366.
[2] *New England Judged*, pp. 74, 75.

whose names are under-written, to the house of correction in Boston, although the Lord, the righteous Judge of Heaven and Earth, is our witness that we have done nothing worthy of stripes or of bonds; and we being committed by your court to be dealt withal as the law provides for foreign Quakers, as ye please to term us; and having some of us suffered your law and pleasures, now that which we do expect is, That whereas we have suffered your law, so now to be set free by the same law as your manner is with strangers, and not to put us in upon the account of one law, and execute another law upon us, of which according to your own manner we were never convicted, as the law expresses: If you had sent us upon the account of your new law, we should have expected the jailer's order to have been on that account, which that it was not, appears by the warrant which we have, and the punishment which we bare, as four of us were whipped, among whom was one that had formerly been whipped; so now also, according to your former law. Friends, let it not be a small thing in your eyes, the exposing, as much as in you lies, our families to ruine. It's not unknown to you, the season and the time of the year, for those that live of husbandry, and what their cattle and families may be exposed unto; and also such as live on trade: We know if the spirit of Christ did dwell and rule in you these things would take impression on your spirits. What our lives and conversations have been in that place is well known; and what we now suffer for, is much for false reports, and ungrounded jealousies of *heresy* and *sedition*. These things lie upon us to lay before you: As for our parts, we have true peace and rest in the Lord in all our sufferings, and are made willing in the power and strength of God, freely to offer up our lives in this cause of God, for which we suffer: Yea, and we do find (through grace) the enlargements of God in our imprisoned state, to whome alone we commit ourselves and families, for the disposing of us according to his infinite wisdom and pleasure, in whose love is our rest and life.

    Laurence⎫
    Cassandra⎬ Southick.
    Josiah⎭
    Samuel Shattuck.
    Joshua Buffum.

From the house of bondage in Boston, wherein we are made captives by the wills of men, although made free by the Son. John 8–36. In which we quietly rest, this 16th of the 5mo, 1658.

A BRIEF SKETCH OF THE SUFFERINGS OF ELIZABETH HOOTEN, AS RELATED IN SEWEL'S HISTORY OF THE QUAKERS, 383–385.

The usage Elizabeth Hooten met with, I can't pass by in silence, because of her age, being about sixty, who hearing of the wickedness committed by those of New-England, was moved to make a voyage to America.

In order thereto she went from England in the

year 1661, having one Joan Broksup with her, a woman near as aged as herself, who freely resolved to be her companion: and because they could not find a master of a ship that was willing to carry them to New-England, because of the fine for every Quaker that was brought thither, they set sail towards Virginia, where they met with a ketch which carried them part of the way, and then they went the rest by land, and so at length came to Boston. But there they could not soon find a place of reception, because of the penalty on those that received a Quaker into their houses. Yet at length a woman received them. Next day they went to the prison to visit their friends; but the gaoler altogether unwilling to let them in, carried them to the Governor Endicot, who, with much scurrilous language, called them 'witches,' and asked Elizabeth, 'what she came for?' to which she answered, 'To do the will of him that sent me.' And he demanded, 'what was that?' she replied, 'To warn thee of shedding any more innocent blood.' To which he returned, 'that he would hang more yet;' but she told him, 'he was in the hand of the Lord, who could take him away first.' This so displeased him, that he sent them to prison, where many more of their friends were. After consultation what to do with them, they were carried two days' journey into the wilderness, among wolves and bears: but by Providence they got to Rhode-Island, where they took ship for Barbados, and from thence to New-England again, and so they returned to Boston. But then they were put into a ship which carried them to Virginia, from whence Elizabeth departed to Old England, where she staid some time in her own habitation.

But it came upon her to visit New-England again; and so she did, taking her daughter Elizabeth along with her. And being arrived, those of the magistrates that were present, would have fined the master of the ship an hundred pounds for bringing her over contrary to their law. But he telling them, that Elizabeth had been with the king, and that she had liberty from him to come thither to buy her a house, this so puzzled these snarling persecutors, that they found themselves at a loss, and thus were stopped from seizing the master's goods.

Elizabeth being come to Boston, notwithstanding the rulers, went to them, and signified that she came thither 'to buy a house for herself to live in.' She was four times at the court for that purpose, but it was denied her: and though she said, 'that this denial would give her occasion, if she went to England again, to lay it before the king,' it was in vain, and had no influence upon them.

Departing then, and passing through several places, she came to Cambridge, and was thrust into a stinking dungeon, where there was nothing to lie down on or sit on. Here they kept her two days and two nights, without affording her anything to eat or drink; and because a certain man in compassion brought her a little milk, he was also cast into prison, and fined five pounds. Being brought to the court, they ordered her to be sent out of their coasts, and to be whipped at three towns, with ten stripes at each. So at Cambridge she was tied to the whipping-post, and lashed with ten stripes, with a three-stringed whip, with three knots at an end: At Watertown she had ten stripes more with willow rods; and to make up all, at Dedham, in a cold frosty morning, she received ten cruel lashes at a cart's tail. And being thus beaten and torn, she was put on horse-back, and carried many miles into the wilderness; and towards night they left her there, where were many wolves, bears, and other wild beasts, and many deep waters to pass through: but being preserved by an invisible hand, she came in the morning into a town called Rehoboth, being neither weary nor faint; and from thence she went to Rhode-Island, where coming to her friends, she gave thanks to God, for having counted her worthy, and enabled her to suffer for his name-sake, beyond what her age and sex, morally speaking, could otherwise have borne.

After some stay there, she returned to Cambridge, about eighty miles, to fetch her linen and clothes, which the inhuman persecutors would not suffer her to take with her when they had whipped her. Having fetched these things, and going back with her daughter and Sarah Coleman, an ancient woman, she was taken up by the

APPENDIX. 181

constable of Charlestown, and carried prisoner to Cambridge; where being asked by one of the magistrates whose name was Daniel Goggin, 'wherefore she came thither, seeing they had warned her not to come there any more:' she answered, 'that she came not there of her own accord, but was forced thither; after she had been to fetch her clothes, which they would not let her take with her when she was whipped, and sent away; but that now returning back she was taken up by force out of the highway, and carried thither.' Then the other old woman was asked, 'whether she owned Elizabeth and her religion?' to which she answered, 'she owned the Truth.' And of Elizabeth's daughter he demanded, 'Dost thou own thy mother's religion?' To which she was silent. And yet they were sent to the house of correction, with order to be whipped. Next morning the executioner came betimes before it was light, and asked them, 'whether they would be whipped there?' which made Elizabeth ask, 'whether he was come to take away their blood in the dark?' and 'whether they were ashamed that their deeds should be seen:' But not heeding what she said, he took her down stairs, and whipped her with a three-stringed whip. Then he brought down the ancient woman, and did the like to her. And taking Elizabeth's daughter he gave the like to her also, who never was there before, nor had said or done anything. After this Elizabeth the mother was whipped again at a cart's-tail at Boston and other places, where she came to see her friends ; since which I have several times seen her in England in a good condition.

ORDER FOR SENDING QUAKERS OUT OF THE JURISDICTION.[1]

Jtt is Ordered that all the Quake^{r}s now in prison. except the persons Condemned to be whip^t be acquainted wth the new lawe made against them and forthwith released from prison and sent from Constable to Constable out of this Jurisdiction and Jf they or any of them be found after twelve howres wthin the same he or they shall be proceeded wth according to the lawe made this present Court. The magis^{ts} haue past this wth Reference to the Consent of theire brethren the dep^{t}s hereto

EDW RAWSON Secret

7 *June*, 1661.

The Deputyes Consent hereto, withall Desireing that Browne & Peirson may ptake of the same liberty with the rest, Desireing o^r Honord Magists Consent hereto

The magis^{t}s Consent not Edw Rawson Secret, but Agree y^t ye 2 psons shall only be whip^t at ye Carts tayle in Boston not exceeding twenty stripes & so dischardged wth ye Rest if theire brethren the Depu^{t}s consent hereto

EDW RAWSON Secret

Consented to by the Deputyes
W^M TORREY Cleric

[1] Massachusetts Archives, vol. x. p. 273.

This order was issued under the fear of interference by the Crown.[1] Samuel Shattuck, who had been banished upon pain of death if he returned, was now in England, and with others had petitioned the King to "restrain the violence of these Rulers of New-England." The petition may be found in vol. i. of Besse's "Collection of Sufferings," where it is given as follows: —

A Declaration of some Part of the Sufferings of the People of God in Scorn called Quakers, from the Professors in New-England, only for the Exercise of their Consciences to the Lord, and obeying and confessing to the Truth, as in his Light he had discovered it to them.

1. Two honest and innocent Women *stripped stark naked*, and searched after such an inhuman manner, as modesty will not permit particularly to mention.

2. *Twelve* strangers in that Country, but free-born of this Nation, received *Twenty-three Whippings*, the most of them being with a Whip of *Three Cords* with *Knots at the Ends*, and laid on with as much Strength as could be by the Arm of their Executioner, the Stripes amounting to *Three Hundred* and *Seventy*.

3. *Eighteen* Inhabitants of the Country, being free-born *English*, received *Twenty three Whippings*, the Stripes amounting to *Two Hundred* and *Fifty*.

4. *Sixty Four Imprisonments* of the Lord's

---

[1] Sewel, Besse, and others, confirm this statement.

People, for their Obedience to his Will, amounting to *Five Hundred* and *Nineteen Weeks*, much of it being very cold Weather, and the Inhabitants kept in Prison in Harvest-time, which was very much to their Loss; besides many more imprisoned, of which Time we cannot give a just-Account.

5. *Two* beaten with *Pitched Ropes*, the blows amounting to an *Hundred* and *Thirty nine*, by which one of them was brought near unto Death, much of his Body being beaten *like unto a Jelly*, and one of their Doctors, a Member of their Church, who saw him, said, *It would be a Miracle if ever he recovered, he expecting the Flesh should rot off the Bones*, who afterwards was *banished upon pain of Death*. There are many Witnesses of this there.

6. Also an Innocent Man, an Inhabitant of *Boston*, they *banished* from his Wife and Children, and put to seek an Habitation in the Winter, and in Case he returned again, he was to be kept Prisoner during his Life, and for returning again he was put in Prison, and hath been now a Prisoner above a year.

7. *Twenty Five Banishments* upon the Penalties of being *whipt*, or having their *Ears cut*, or *branded in the Hand*, if they returned.

8. *Fines* laid upon the Inhabitants for meeting together, and edifying one another, as the Saints ever did; and for refusing to Swear, it being contrary to Christ's Command, amounting to about a *Thousand Pounds*, beside what they

APPENDIX. 185

have done since that we have not heard of, many Families, in which there are many Children, are almost ruined by their unmerciful Proceedings.

9. *Five* kept *Fifteen Days* in all, *without Food*, and *Fifty Eight Days* shut up close by the Gaoler, and had none that he knew of; and from some of them he stopt up the Windows, hindring them from convenient Air.

10. *One* laid *Neck and Heels* in Irons for *Sixteen Hours*.

11. *One* very deeply *burnt* in the *Right-Hand* with the Letter (H) after he had been *whipt* with above *Thirty Stripes*.

12. *One chained* to a *Log* of *Wood* the *most Part* of *Twenty Days*, in an open Prison, in the Winter-time.

13. *Five* Appeals to *England* denied at *Boston*.

14. *Three* had their *Right Ears cut by the Hangman in the Prison*, the Door being barred, and not a Friend suffered to be present while it was doing, though some much desired it.

15. *One* of the Inhabitants of *Salem*, who since is *banished upon Pain* of *Death*, had *one Half of his House and Land seized on while he was in Prison*, a Month before he knew of it.

16. At a General Court in *Boston* they made an Order, *That those who had not where-withall* to answer the Fines that were laid upon them for their Consciences, *should be sold for Bondmen and Bondwomen* to Barbadoes, Virginia, *or any of the* English *Plantations.*

17. *Eighteen* of the People of God were at several Times *banished upon pain of Death*; six of them were their own Inhabitants, two of which being very aged People, and well known among their Neighbours to be of honest Conversation, being banished from their Houses and Families, and put upon Travelling and other Hardships, soon ended their Days, whose Death we can do no less than charge upon the Rulers of *Boston*, they being the Occasion of it.

18. Also *Three* of the Servants of the Lord *they put to Death*, all of them for Obedience to the Truth, in the Testimony of it, against the Wicked Rulers and Laws at *Boston*.

19. And since they have *banished Four more upon Pain of Death*, and *Twenty Four* of the Inhabitants of *Salem* were presented, and more *Fines* called for, and their Goods seized on to the Value of *Forty Pounds* for meeting together in the Fear of God, and some for refusing to Swear.

These Things, O King! from Time to Time have we patiently suffered, and not for the Transgression of any just or righteous Law, either pertaining to the Worship of God, or the Civil Government of *England*, but simply and barely for our Consciences to God, of which we can more at large give thee, or whom thou mayst order, a full account (if thou will let us have Admission to thee, who are *banished upon Pain of Death*, and have had our *Ears cut*, who are some of us in *England* attending upon thee) both of the *Causes of our Sufferings*, and the *Manner of their disorderly and illegal Proceedings against us;* they began with *Immodesty*, went on in *Inhumanity* and *Cruelty*, and were not satisfied until they had the *Blood of Three of the Martyrs of Jesus:* Revenge for all which we do not seek, but lay them before thee, considering thou hast been well acquainted with Sufferings, and so mayst the better consider them that suffer, and mayst for the future restrain the Violence of these Rulers of *New-England*, having Power in thy Hands, they being but the Children of the Family of which thou art Chief Ruler, who have in divers their Proceedings *forfeited their Patent*, as upon strict Enquiry in many Particulars will appear.

And this, O King! we are assured of, that in Time to come it will not repent thee, if by a close Rebuke thou stoppest the *Bloody Proceedings* of these *Bloody Persecutors*, for in so doing thou wilt engage the Hearts of many honest People unto thee both there and here, and for such Works of Mercy the Blessing is obtained; and showing it is the Way to prosper: We are Witnesses of these Things, who

Besides *many long Imprisonments*, and *many cruel Whippings*, had our *Ears cut*,

JOHN ROUSE
JOHN COPELAND.

Besides *many long Imprisonments, divers cruel Whippings*, with the *seizing on our Goods*, are *banished upon Pain of Death*, and some of us do wait here in *England*, and desire that we may have an Order to return in Peace to our Families,

SAMUEL SHATTOCK   JOSIAH SOUTHICK
NICHOLAS PHELPS   JOSEPH NICHOLSON
JANE NICHOLSON

Commenting upon the above petition, Besse says:—

" This representation of their case to the King, with the earnest and incessant solicitations of Edward Burrough, and others, on their behalf, procured a Mandamus from that Monarch by which an effectual stop was put to the proceedings in New-England of putting men to death for Religion, by which their blind zeal and fury would otherwise probably have destroyed many innocent people. Nevertheless they yet continued by cruel whippings, and other barbarities to demonstrate that they repented not of their former cruelty, but that they were restricted by force of the Kings authority, and not from any alteration in their own tempers or inclinations, as will plainly appear by the narrative of their proceedings."

It is probable that Besse is not entirely accurate in stating that the presentation of this petition " procured a Mandamus," though it doubtless prepared the way for one. When it was presented the news of the execution of Leddra at Boston had not reached England. Sewel, who is an

APPENDIX.

earlier authority than Besse, states that the king had seen a copy of George Bishop's account of the "cruel persecution," and was so much affected by it that he resolved to interfere. His resolve was soon after confirmed by the "news of William Leddra's death." Edward Burrough having obtained an audience, said to the king, "There was a vein of innocent blood opened in his dominions, which if it were not stopped, would overrun all." To which he replied, "But I will stop that vein." The Mandamus was granted forthwith, and Shattuck was empowered to carry it to Boston. Whittier's poem, "The King's Missive," makes it unnecessary to repeat here a detailed account of Shattuck's arrival, for this poem is, or should be, in every American household. The reception of the Missive by the Massachusetts authorities placed them in a dilemma. They dare not obey the command to send the prisoners to England for trial,[1] nor could they proceed with the cases in their own court. There was but one course left by which they could avoid a conflict with the Crown. Hitherto, gaol deliveries implied scourging and banishment of Quaker prisoners. For once, it was necessary to forego these pious festivities. Prosecution and persecution must be suspended temporarily; such Quakers as were in gaol must be set at liberty. An order for their unconditional release and discharge was issued. Sewel gives

[1] The Quakers had repeatedly appealed to be sent to England for trial.

the text of the Royal Mandamus, and the order for the release of the Friends, as follows: —

Charles R.

Trusty and Well-beloved, We Greet you well. Having been informed that several of Our subjects amongst you, called Quakers, have been, and are Imprisoned by you, whereof some have been Executed, and others (as hath been represented unto us) are in danger to undergo the like : we have thought fit to signify our pleasure in that behalf, for the future ; and do hereby require, that if there be any of those people called Quakers amongst you, now already condemned to suffer death, or other corporal punishment, or that are imprisoned, and obnoxious to the like condemnation, you are to forbear to proceed any further therein ; but that you forthwith send the said persons (whether condemned or imprisoned) over into this our kingdom of England, together with the respective crimes or offenses laid to their charge ; to the end that such course may be taken with them here, as shall be agreeable to our laws, and their demerits. And for so doing, these our letters shall be your sufficient warrant and discharge. *Given at our court at Whitehall, the 9th day of September, 1661, in the 13th year of our reign.*

By his majesty's command,

WILLIAM MORRIS.

The superscription was, " To our Trusty and

Well-beloved, John Endicot, Esq. and to all and every other the governor, or governors, of our plantations of New-England, and of all the colonies thereunto belonging, that now are, or hereafter shall be; and to all and every the ministers and officers of our said plantation and colonies whatsoever, within the continent of New-England."

Orders for Release and Discharge of Quaker Prisoners.[1]

"*To William Salter, keeper of the prison at Boston:*

You are required by authority, and order of the general court, forthwith to release and discharge the Quakers, who at present are in your custody. See that you don't neglect this.

By order of the court,

EDWARD RAWSON, *Secretary.*"

BOSTON, *the 9th of December,* 1661.

A Quaker jubilation[2] followed this gaol delivery, but the liberty they enjoyed was of short duration. Fear of further interference from England having been allayed, the law of May 22, 1661, with slight modification, was reënacted. This was done on the 8th of October, 1662. The fires of persecution were rekindled. John Endicott pursued the Friends with relentless cruelty until, in March, 1665, death ended his wicked and bloody career.

[1] Sewel, p. 321. [2] Besse, vol. ii. p. 226.

APPENDIX.

Bellingham succeeded Endicott, but was less persistent, and instances of cruelty, under his administration, are not numerous. His clemency was due in part to the interference of royal commissioners, who, on the 24th of May, 1665, submitted a series of demands to the General Court, one of which was, that the Quakers should be allowed to attend to their secular business without molestation.[1] Bellingham died in December, 1672. In November, 1675, persecution was revived by the passage of a law prohibiting Quaker meetings,[2] and in May, 1677, it was further provided, that the constables should "make diligent search" for such meetings, and should "break open any door where peaceable entrance is denied them."[3] For a brief period it seemed as if the scenes of 1661 and 1662 were to be reenacted. Men and women were seized, dragged to gaol, imprisoned, fed on bread and water, fined, and publicly whipped. In the 6th month (August) fourteen Quakers were taken at one meeting, and in the following week a second arrest of fifteen was made. Most, if not all of them, in addition to other punishment, suffered flogging at the whipping post. These are the latest cases of corporal punishment noted by Besse. The Friends rallied in increasing numbers and once more the authorities were forced to respect their rights. It was during this period of excitement that Margaret Brewster was ap-

[1] *Mass. Records*, vol. iv. p. 212.
[2] *Ibid*. vol. v. p. 60.   [3] *Ibid*. p. 134.

prehended for the performance of an act which, however peculiar or fanatical it may be considered, was refined and dignified as compared with the brutal indecency of the Court when she was on trial. The following report of the trial will well repay the reading. It is worth remarking that while Margaret Brewster furnishes Puritan apologists with most productive capital, no one of them has yet acknowledged the obligation by naming the cause of her performance, the circumstances attending it, the conduct of her judges, or the punishment meted out to her.

Trial, or Examination, of Margaret Brewster, and others, at the Court in Boston, on the 4th of the Sixth Month, 1677.[1]

Clerk. Margaret Brewster

M. B. Here.

Clerk. Are you the Woman?

M. B. Yes, I am the Woman.

Governour.[2] Read the Mittimus.

The Mittimus was read.

Governour, to the People. What have you to lay to her Charge?

Constable. If this be the Woman, I don't know; for she was then in the Shape of a Devil: I thought her hair had been a Perriwigg, but it was her own Hair.

The Constable said more, but so faintly and low as not to be understood.

[1] Besse, vol. ii. pp. 261-265.
[2] John Leverett.

Gov. You hear your Accusation.

M. B. I do not hear it.

Gov. Are you the Woman that came into Mr. Thatcher's Meeting-house with your Hair fruzled, and dressed in the Shape of a Devil?

M. B. I am the Woman that came into Priest Thatcher's House of Worship with my Hair about my Shoulders, Ashes upon my Head, my Face coloured black, and Sackcloth upon my upper Garments.

Gov. You own yourself to be the Woman.

M. B. Yea, I do.

Gov. What made you come so?

M. B. I came in Obedience to the Lord.

Gov. The Lord! The Lord never sent you, for you came like a Devil, and in the Shape of a Devil incarnate.

M. B. Noble Governour! Thy Name is spread in other Parts of the World for a moderate Man, now I desire thee and thy Assistants to hear me with Patience, that I may give an Account of my so coming among you.

Gov. Too moderate for such as you: But go on.

M. B. The Lord God of Heaven and Earth, the Maker and Creator of all Man kind, laid this Service upon me more than three Years ago to visit this bloody Town of Boston.

Here some spake to the Governour to stop her from speaking any more; but the Governour said, Let her go on.

M. B. And when the appointed Time drew

APPENDIX. 195

near, the Lord pleased to visit me with Sickness, before I could clearly give up to this Service, and as I may say, I was raised as one from the Dead, and came from my sick Bed to visit the bloody Town of Boston, and to bear a living Testimony for the God of my Life, and go as a Sign among you; and as I gave up to this Service, my Sickness went away. It is said the Prophet Jonah was three Days in the Whale's Belly, but I could compare my Condition to nothing, but as if I had been in the Belly of Hell for many Weeks, and I think I may so say for some Months, until I gave up to this Service; and now if you be suffered to take away my Life, I am very well contented.

Gov. You shall escape with your Life.

Simon Broadstreet. You are a Blasphemer.

M. B. I have not blasphemed.

S. Broadstreet. I cannot believe what you say to be true.

M. B. Canst thou not believe? Well, I am sorry thou canst not believe.

Gov. Are you a married Woman?

M. B. I am.

Gov. Did your Husband give Consent to your Coming?

M. B. Yea, he did.

Gov. Have you any Thing to shew under his Hand?

M. B. He gave his Consent before many Witnesses in Barbadoes, and said, He did believe this Service was of God, and he durst not withstand it, but was willing to give me up to this Service, as many in Barbadoes can witness; and now, if you be suffered to take away my Life, I can now lay down my Head in Peace, for I have thus far done what the Lord required at my Hands, and am clear of the Blood of all People in this Place, so far as I know; and the Desire of my Soul is, that it may be with this Town as it was with Nineveh of old, for when the Lord sent his Prophet Jonah to cry against Nineveh, it is said, They put on Sackcloth, and covered their Heads with Ashes, and repented, and the Lord withdrew his Judgments for forty Years: And my Soul cries to the Lord that this People may repent, that the Lord may spare them yet forty Years: For it was in true Obedience to the Lord, and in Love to your Souls, that I was made to come as a Sign amongst you, for I feel that in my Heart at this Moment, that I could even give up my Life, to be sacrificed for the Good of your Souls. I have nothing but Love in my Heart to the worst of my Enemies here in this Town.

Gov. Hold, hold Woman, you run too fast. Silence in the Court.

M. B. Governour! I desire thee to hear me a little, for I have something to say in Behalf of my Friends in this Place: I desire thee and thine Assistants to put an End to these cruel Laws that you have made to prosecute my Friends for meeting together to worship the True and Living God. Oh Governour! I cannot but press thee again and again, to put an End to these cruel Laws that you have made to fetch my Friends from their peaceable Meetings, and keep them three Days in the House of Correction, and then whip them for worshipping the True and Living God: Governour! Let me entreat thee to put an End to these Laws, for the Desire of my Soul is, that you may act for God, and then would you prosper, but if you act against the Lord and his blessed Truth, you will assuredly come to nothing, the Mouth of the Lord hath spoken it, for if you will draw your Swords against the Lord and his People, the Lord will assuredly draw his Sword against you; for there never was any Weapon formed against God and his blessed Truth that ever prospered: It's my Testimony for the Lord God of my Life.

Gov. Hold Woman. Call Lydia Wright.

Clerk. Call Lydia Wright of Long-Island.

L. Wright. Here.

Gov. Are you one of the Women that came in with this Woman into Mr. Thatcher's Meeting-house to disturb him at his Worship?

L. W. I was; but I disturbed none, for I came in peaceably, and spake not a Word to Man, Woman, or Child.

Gov. What came you for then?

L. W. Have you not made a Law that we should come to your Meeting? For we were peaceably met together at our own Meeting-house, and some of your Constables came in, and haled some of our Friends out, and said, This is not a

Place for you to worship God in. Then we asked him, Where we should worship God? Then they said, We must come to your publick Worship. And upon the First-day following I had something upon my Heart to come to your publick Worship, when we came in peaceably, and spake not a Word, yet we were haled to Prison, and there have been kept near a month.

S. Broadstreet. Did you come there to hear the Word?

L. W. If the Word of God was there, I was ready to hear it.

Gov. Did your Parents give Consent you should come thither?

L. W. Yes, my Mother did.

Gov. Shew it.

L. W. If you will stay till I can send Home, I will engage to get from under my Mother's Hand, that she gave her Consent.

Juggins, a Magistrate, said, You are led by the Spirit of the Devil, to ramble up and down the Country, like Whores and Rogues a Caterwawling.

L. W. Such Words do not become those who call themselves Christians, for they that sit to Judge for God in Matters of Conscience, ought to be sober and serious, for Sobriety becomes the People of God, for these are a weighty and ponderous People.

Gov. Did you own this Woman?

L. W. I own her, and have Unity with her, and I do believe so have all the faithful Servants of the Lord, for I know the Power and Presence of the Lord was with us.

Juggins. You are mistaken: You do not know the Power of God; you are led by the Spirit and Light within you, which is of the Devil: There is but one God, and you do not worship that God which we worship.

L. W. I believe thou speakest Truth, for if you worshipped that God which we worship, you would not persecute his People, for we worship the God of Abraham, Isaac, and Jacob, and the same God that Daniel worshipped.

So they cried, Take her away.

Then Mary Miles was called.

Clerk. Mary Miles of Black-point.

M. M. I am here.

Gov. Do you live at Black-point?

M. M. Nay: My former Living was there, but my outward Living is now at Salem, when I am at Home.

Gov. Are you a married Woman?

M. M. Nay, I am not married.

Gov. Did you come into Mr. Thatcher's Meeting-house with this Woman that had a black Face?

M. M. Yea, I did.

Gov. What was the Cause?

M. M. My Freedom was in the Lord, and in Obedience to his Will, and the Unity of his Spirit, I came.

Gov. So, so, then you had Unity with her, it seems, but you had not Communion with her, for you had not a black Face.

M. M. I had good Unity with her, and do believe, and witness, and bear my Testimony for the Lord, that it was his Work and Service that she went in; therefore I had Unity and Fellowship with her, and the Lord in his due Time will reveal and manifest his own Work.

Gov. Hold your Tongue, you prating Housewife; you are led by the Spirit of the Devil to run about the Country a wandring, like Whores and Rogues.

M. M. They that are led by the Spirit of God deny the Works of the Devil: The Earth is the Lord's and the Fulness thereof; and he can command his Servants to go wheresoever he pleaseth to send them; and none can hinder his Power, for it is unlimited.

Cryer. Take them away, and carry them to Prison.

M. M. Yea, I am made willing to go to Prison, and to Death, if it were required of me to seal the Testimony of Jesus with my Blood, as some of my Friends and Brethren have done, whose Blood you have shed, which cries to the Lord for Vengeance, and the Cry will not cease till Vengeance come upon you.

Then Barbara Bowers was called.

Margaret Brewster answered, Barbara Bowers was not concerned with us in this Service.

Gov. Let us hear what she says.

B. Bowers. I was in the Meeting-house, but did not go in with them.

Then they were all carried to Prison again,

and about an Hour after brought again into the Court, when the Governour being present, the Clerk read the Sentence as follows, viz.

Margaret Brewster, You are to have your Clothes stript off to the Middle, and to be tied to a Cart's Tail at the South Meeting-house, and to be drawn through the Town, and to receive twenty Stripes upon your naked Body.

M. B. The Will of the Lord be done: I am contented.

The Clerk proceeded, saying, Lydia Wright and Mary Miles, You are to be tied to the Cart's Tail also. Barbara Bowers, you are to be tied also.

M. Brewster. I told the Court before, that Barbara was not concerned with us in the Service, and therefore I desire you may remit her Sentence; for I knew not of her Coming with us, neither did I see her with us, till we came into the Common-Gaol: Therefore I desire she may not suffer.

Gov. Take her away.

Gaoler. I am loth to pull you.

M. B. I will go without pulling, and go as chearfully as Daniel went to the Lion's Den, for the God of Daniel is with me; and the God of Abraham, Isaac, and Jacob, goes along with me: The same God that was with the three Children in the fiery Furnace goes with me now; and I am glad that I am worthy to be a Sufferer in this Bloody Town, and to be numbred amongst my dearly and well-beloved Brethren and Sisters, that sealed their Testimonies with their Blood.

So they were carried to Prison again, this being the Seventh-day of the Week; and on the Fifth day following, the Sentence was executed.

During the Examination of these Women, they appeared altogether unconcerned as to themselves, being fully resigned to whatsoever Sufferings might be their Portion; stedfastly maintaining their full Assurance of a divine Call to the Service they went upon, and a perfect Peace and Serenity of Mind in yielding Obedience thereunto: In all which they seem to have really exercised the Faith and Patience of the Saints and People of God.

ABSTRACT FROM JOINT LETTER OF WILLIAM ROBINSON AND MARMADUKE STEVENSON.[1]

We that are Free-born English-men, we demand our Liberty for the Exercise of our pure Consciences in this Country, as well as other English-men; we being Free-born English-men, we may, by the Law of God, claim our Liberty before many other People: We who are not Transgressors of the Law of God, neither of any Law or Decree that is according thereunto, What is the Reason that we should be Banished upon Death, out of your Jurisdiction, more than

[1] *New England Judged*, pp. 252–259.

any other People? What, is it because we are Turners of the World upside-down? What, is it because we are termed Ring-leaders of a People, that are, in Scorn, called Quakers? What, is it because the Laws of our God, which we Obey, are different from all the Unrighteous and Bloody Laws of New England? What, is it because we cannot Obey the Commandment of the Rulers of New England, that have commanded us to Bow to the Spirit that ruled in Haman, which now rules in these bloody Rulers of Boston, and elsewhere in New England? Nay, I say, the Lord our God hath Raised, and is Raising, the Royal Seed and Spirit that ruled in Mordecai, that could not, nor cannot Stoop nor Bow to the Spirit that ruleth in proud Haman: I say, see and behold, if the same Spirit rules not in you, ye Rulers, Chief Priests, and Inhabitants of Boston and elsewhere. . . . Are not you preparing a Gallows to Hang us thereon, as Haman did for Mordecai? But, take heed, We Warn you in the Name of the Lord God, consider what you are going to do: In the Name of the Lord we demand, that we may have Liberty, for the Exercise of our pure Consciences, within your Jurisdiction, as well as other English-men, seeing that you cannot lay to our Charge, the Transgression of any Law of God, we being Men that Fear the Lord God of Heaven and Earth; and we come not for any Thing of yours, God is our Witness; it is not for any Thing that you have, that we come for; for we do not lack any outward Thing; for many of us have both Houses and Land of our own, and Silver also, in Old England, so that we seek not any Thing that you have (God is our Witness, whom we Serve in the Spirit of Truth, who hath constrained us to leave all, and to follow him) that it is not the World (that doth perish with the handling thereof) that we seek or labour for, but the Good and Eternal Welfare of the Sons of Men: For the Seed's sake, which is Oppressed in New England, and other parts of the World, do we Labour, and Travel, and Suffer all manner of Hardships: For Christ's sake are we become Fools, and do Suffer all manner of Evil to be done unto us. Christ said unto his Disciples, They shall do all manner of Evil to you, for my Name sake; but those that did it, and those that do it, know neither God, nor his Son Jesus Christ, neither have they the Love of God abiding in them: . . . It is written in the Warrant, whereby we were Committed to Prison, That we shall be Tryed according to Law. We desire no more, than to be Tryed according to Equity, Truth, and true Judgment, to be Tryed according to the Law of God; but your Law, you unjust Men, we deny to be Tryed by it; for you are both our Accusers and Judges; which is not according to the Law of God: For, Equity and Truth Judgeth and Condemneth all unsound Judgment, Unrighteousness, Partiality and Respecting of Persons. . . . This is a Warning to you all in New-England, who have had a Hand in persecuting the Saints and Children of the Lord (who are by you, in Scorn and Contempt, called Quakers). Give over your Cruelty; cease from Oppressing the Innocent; for the Lord God hath regard unto their Sufferings, and the Lord God is Risen, and Arising, to plead their Cause against all their Enemies, and all their Adversaries must fall before them; for the Lord is with them, and the Shout of a Mighty Prince is among the Innocent People, called Quakers; and this is the Day of their Suffering, and the Day of your Cruelties and Persecution upon them, within this New-England: But the Day of their Deliverance draweth near, and the Day wherein they shall Rejoyce in the Lord, the God of their Salvation, who is mighty to Save, and able to Deliver them out of the Hands, and out of the Mouths of Devourers, and from the Jaws of the Ungodly and Cruel Men; who will take Vengeance at that Day upon all bloody-minded Men and blind Persecutors: And at that Day you shall find that the Lord will be too hard for you, tho' you now Boast in your Wickedness. And thus far I am Clear, and have cleared my Conscience to you at this time: And whether you will hear, or forbear, I am clear of your Blood: I who am now a Sufferer under you, with my Brother and Companion, whose Lives are not dear unto us, to lay them down as a Witness against such a Bloody, and Unrighteous, and Hypocritical Generation:

And this we are ready to Seal with our Blood, for the breaking of your Bloody Law.

From us, who are in Scorn called Quakers, who are Sufferers under Zions Oppressors. The 6th Month, 1659.
In the Common Gaol, in the Bloody Town of Boston.

WILLIAM ROBINSON.
MARMADUKE SEVENSON.

LETTER OF MARY DYER.[1]

The 28th of the 8th Month, 1659.

Once more to the general court assembled in Boston, speaks Mary Dyar, even as before: my life is not accepted, neither availeth me, in comparison of the lives and liberty of the truth and servants of the living God, for which in the bowels of love and meekness I sought you: yet, nevertheless, with wicked hands have you put two of them to death, which makes me to feel, that the mercies of the wicked are cruelty; I rather choose to die than to live, as from you, as guilty of their innocent blood: therefore seeing my request is hindered, I leave you to the righteous Judge, and searcher of all hearts, who, with the pure measure of light he hath given to every man to profit withal, will in his due time let you see whose servants you are, and of whom you have taken counsel, which I desire you to search into: but all his counsel hath been slighted, and

[1] Sewel's *History of the Quakers*, p. 265.

you would none of his reproofs. Read your portion, Prov. i. 24 to 32. For verily the night cometh on you apace, wherein no man can work, in which you shall assuredly fall to your own master. In obedience to the Lord, whom I serve with my spirit, and pity to your souls, which you neither know nor pity, I can do no less than once more to warn you, to put away the evil of your doings, and kiss the son, the light in you, before his wrath be kindled in you; for where it is, nothing without you can help or deliver you out of his hand at all; and if these things be not so, then say, 'there hath been no prophet from the Lord sent amongst you.' Though we be nothing, yet it is his pleasure, by things that are not, to bring to naught things that are.

When I heard your last order read, it was a disturbance unto me, that was so freely offering up my life to him that gave it me, and sent me hither so to do, which obedience being his own work, he gloriously accompanied with his presence, and peace, and love in me, in which I rested from my labour; till by your order and the people, I was so far disturbed, that I could not retain any more of the words thereof, than that I should return to prison, and there remain forty and eight hours; to which I submitted, finding nothing from the Lord to the contrary, that I may know what his pleasure and counsel is concerning me, on whom I wait therefore, for he is my life, and the length of my days; and as I said before, I came at his command, and go at his command.   MARY DYAR.

ABSTRACT OF LETTER FROM WILLIAM LEDDRA WRITTEN TO HIS FRIENDS ON THE DAY BEFORE HIS EXECUTION.[1]

Most dear and inwardly beloved,

The sweet influences of the Morning-Star, like a flood distilling into my innocent habitation, hath so filled me with the joy of the Lord in the beauty of holiness, that my spirit, is as if it did not inhabit a tabernacle of clay, but is wholly swallowed up in the bosom of eternity, from whence it had its being.

Alas, alas, what can the wrath and spirit of man, that lusteth to envy, aggravated by the heat and strength of the king of the locusts, which came out of the pit, do unto one that is hid in the secret places of the Almighty? Or unto them that are gathered under the healing wings of the prince of peace? under whose armour of light they shall be able to stand in the day of trial, having on the breast-plate of righteousness, and the sword of the spirit, which is their weapon of war against spiritual wickedness, principalities and powers, and the rulers of the darkness of this world, both within and without! Oh, my beloved! I have waited as a dove at the windows of the ark, and have stood still in that watch, which the Master, (without whom I could do nothing) did at his coming reward with fulness of his love, wherein my heart did rejoice, that I might in the love and life of God, speak a few

[1] Sewel, p. 312.

words to you sealed with the spirit of promise, that the taste thereof might be a savour of life, to your life, and a testimony in you of my innocent death: and if I had been altogether silent, and the Lord had not opened my mouth unto you, yet he would have opened your hearts, and there have sealed my innocency with the streams of life, by which we are all baptized into that body which is in God, whom, and in whose presence there is life; in which, as you abide, you stand upon the pillar and ground of truth: for, the life being the truth and the way, go not one step without it, lest you should *compass a mountain in the wilderness*; for, *unto everything there is a season.* . . . fear not what they can do unto you: *greater is he that is in you, than he that is in the world:* for he will clothe you with humility, and in the power of his meekness you shall reign over all the rage of your enemies in the favour of God; wherein, as you stand in faith, ye are the salt of the earth; for, many seeing your good works, may glorify God in the day of their visitation.

Take heed of receiving that which you saw not in the light, lest you give ear to the enemy. *Bring all things to the light*, that *they may be proved, whether they be wrought in God;* the love of the world, the lust of the flesh, and the lust of the eye, are without the light, in the world; therefore possess your vessels in all sanctification and honour, and let your eye look at the mark: *he that hath called you is holy:* and if

there be an eye that offends, pluck it out, and cast it from you : let not a temptation take hold, for if you do, it will keep from the favour of God, and that will be a sad state; for, without grace possessed, there is no assurance of salvation : by grace you are saved ; and the witnessing of it is sufficient for you, to which I commend you all, my dear friends, and in it remain,
Your brother,
WILLIAM LEDDRA.
Boston gaol, the 13th of the First Month, 16$\frac{80}{61}$.

DANIEL GOULD'S LETTER.[1]

To the rulers & peopele of the toun & Jurisdiction of bostene.

It is writen in the criptuars wch you say is youar rule, y^t Christ sayed, lern of me. Whear is it writen or declared in the criptuars y^t Christ ever tought or commanded eny to parciquet, to put in prison or to bannish any for thear relegin ; but is it not writen to the contry, & did not he say to his desippels, let them alone, these be blind leders. Now if we wch yee call quakrs be the blind leaders then see if you do not mak it manifest also that you . . . For his desipels obayed his command & let them alowen, but ye do not. Now what doe you exspect to be judged by when your own condems you so plainly. Conseder it well, the blind ledars were them that did not belive in the light but denyed the light and

[1] Massachusetts Archives, vol. x. p. 265.

would clim up sum other way & so be in the wrong way, there foar caled blind leders out of the light. . . . Again consider of whom yee lerne, for Christ said to his desipels, resist not evel, but yee have put in prison & banished them that have dune you no wrong nor thoght eny towards you. And Peter speking of his sufarings, said he left us an exsampell y^t we should follow his steps; now thearfore consider in youer selves & in your secrit chambers lay it to hart and with the true light which will deceive no man, sarch & see in whose steps ye are, whether in the steps of the sufarars or in the steps of the pursiqutars, for I am greved to see your cruelty and your hard hartednes against a peopell that cannot flatar you nor willfully doe you eny wrong, but if any should doe you any wrong or trespas against eny man, let a rightus law take hold of such; but what ned any law be made against the innosent; those y^t doe you noe wrong. . . . Conserning religun lete every one be fully parswaded in his owen mind & worship acording as God shal preswad his owne hart, & if any worship not God as thay ought to doe & yet liveth quietly & pesably with ther naibers & contery men & doth them noe wrong, is it not safar for you to let them aloene to receive thear reward from him who said I will render venganse to myne ennmy^s & reward them that hate me. Let God alone be Lord of the conscience & not man, & let us have the same liburty & freedom amongst yee as other ingleshmen hav to com and visit owar frends & kindered, & doe that wich is honest & lawfal to be done in bying or seling; and if any have amind to reason or spek consarning the way and worship of God, that thay may not be put in prison or punished for it; soe let peopel have libarty to try all thing & hold fast that which is good: I allso desiar you serisly to consider & give me an answar to these towe querys. . . . whether Gallio did well being a deputy, yea or nay, when the Jewse brough Paule to the jidgment seate, saying this felow preswads peopell to worship God contrary to the law, & his ansar was, if it wear a matar of wrong or wicked leudnes to ye Jewes, reason would that I should bear with you, but if it be a questyon of words or names of yor law, lok you to it, for I will be no judg on such matters; & he drove them fram the Judgment seat. Acts the 18th, 13, 14, 15, 16. Whether Gemaliall, being a doctor of law, did councell well, yea or nay, when . . . took counsel to kill the apostels after hee had told them of sume that were scatared & brought to naught, & said, take hede to your selvs of what you intend to doe touching these men and let them alone, for if this counsel or this work be of man it will came to naught but if it be of God yee cannot overthrow it, lest yee be found fighters against God. Read the Acts, 5th, from 33 to 40.   DANNIAL GOULLD

rod Iland the 3 month 1660.

APPENDIX.

LETTER FROM MARY TRASKE AND MARGARET SMITH, ACCUSING THE GOVERNMENT.[1]

To Thee John Indicot & ye rest of ye rulers of this jurisdiction, who are given up to fight agst ye Lord & his truth in this ye day wherein its springing forth, & by ye comlines of it hath ye Lord o^r God constrained us to take up ye cross and to follow him through greate tryalls & sufferings as to ye outward. And herein we can rejoyce y^t we are counted worthy & called hereunto to beare our testimony against a cruell & hard-hearted people who are slighting ye day of yor visitation & foolishly requiting ye Lord for his goodnes, & shamefully intreated his hidden ones whom he hath sent amongst yo^u to call yo^w from ye evill of yor waies, y^t yee might come wth them to partake of his love & feel his life & power in yor owne hearts; y^t with us y^{ee} might have been brought to be subject to ye higher power, Christ Jesus; whom yo^w should have been obedient to and hearkned to his judgments while he stood at ye dore & knocked (for he will not alwaies strive wth man) & then it should have been well wth yo^w. But seing yee are gone from this y^t leadeth into tendernes, love & meeknes, & to doe unto all as yo^w would be done unto; therefore yee are given up unto a Spirit of Error & hardnes of heart & blindnes of mind; ye eye of yor minds being blinded by ye god of this world; so y^t yo^u

[1] Massachusetts Archives, vol. x. p. 267.

cannot se our life wch is hid wth Christ in God, who is become our light & life & hope of glory and our exceeding greate reward; in whom we doe reigne; yea surely ye God of Jacob is wth us w^tever yo^u may be able to say against us: for behold ye Lord our God is arising as a mighty and terrible one to plead ye cause of his people and to cleare ye cause of ye innocent; but surely he will in no wise acquit ye guilty who have shed ye bloud of ye innocent; & yee shall assuredly feel his judgments who have wilfully put forth yor hands against his Chosen; & yee have cut of ye righteous from amongst yo^u & are still taking councell against ye Lord, to proceed against more of his people, but this know, ye Lord our God will confound yor councell & lay your glory in ye dust, & to whom will yo^u flee for help; whither will yo^u goe to hide yor selves; for verely ye Lord will strip of all yor coverings, for yo^u are not covered with ye Spirit of ye Lord, therefore ye wo is gone out against yo^u; for yor place of defence is a refuge of lies & under falsehoods yee have hid your selves; wo: wo: unto yo^u, for yo^u have forsaken ye Lord, ye fountaine of living water, & are greedily swallowing ye poluted waters y^t comes through ye stinking channell of yor hireling masters unclean spirits, whom Christ cries wo against, & who cannot cease from sin, having hearts exercised wth coveteous practices: wo unto them (saith ye scripture) for they have run greedily after ye Error of Balaam who loved ye wages of unrighteousnes; & are seeking inchantments against ye seed of Jacob; but there divinations against Israell ye Lord will confound; and all yor wicked councells bring to nought: wo unto yo^u y^t decree unrighteous decrees & write greiviousnes, y^t yo^u have prescribed to turne away ye poore & needy from there right. Have ye not sold yor selves to worke wickednes, & are strengthning yor selves in your abomination till ye measure of your iniquity be full; surely ye overflowing scourge will pas over yo^u & sweep away yor refuge of lies, & yor covenant wth hell shall be disanulled; for loe, destruction & misery is in yor way & ye way of peace yee doe not know, for yo^u are gone from ye good old way after yor owne waies, therefore ye way of holines is hid from your eyes. O y^t yo^u had owned ye day of yor visitation before it had been to late, & had hearkned to ye voice of his servants whom he hath sent unto yo^u againe & againe in love & tendernes to yor soules; but yo^u would not hearken unto ye Lord when he called, therefore when yo^u cry & call he will not heare yo^u. Although you may call unto him yet he will not answer; he will laugh at yor calamity when it cometh; for yo^u have set at nought all his councell, & have chosen rather to walke in yor owne councell; but this know, y^t if you had hearkned to ye councell of ye Lord (ye light) wch is now yor condemnation, & had waited there to know his will; then yo^u should have knowne it; and then these wicked lawes had never been made nor prosecuted by yo^u, wch yo^u have made in yor

owne wills, contrary to ye law of God, wch is pure and leadeth all y^t yeldeth obedience to it into purity & holines of life. And for our being obedient to this law wch ye Lord hath written in our hearts, we are hated & persecuted by yo^u who are in Cains nature murdering ye just; yea, surely ye cause is ye Lords, for wch we have suffered all this time, & ye battell is ye Lords, & he will arise and stand up for them y^t faithfully beares forth there testimony to ye end. And yee shall be as broken vessels before him which cannot be joyned together againe; therefore feare & tremble before ye Lord, who is coming upon yo^u as a theife in ye night; from whom yo^u shall not be able to hide your selves, & will reward yo^u according to yor workes; whose judgments are just; and he is risen to plead wth unjust rulers preists and people, who are joyned together in a profession of godlines, & glorying in it but denying ye power thereof in them where it apeares; but your glorying will be turned into shame & confusion of face, & yor beauty will be as a fading flower wch suddenly withereth away; & this yo^u shall find to be true in ye day when ye Lord shall accomplish it upon yo^u. And we have written to cleare our conscience, & if yo^u should account us yor enemies for speaking ye truth, & heat ye furnace of our affliction hotter, yet know we shall not fall downe & worship yor wills; neither esteeme all ye dumb idolls, after wch yo^u are led, of no other use but to be throwne aside to ye moles and ye batts, for so is ye shadows (if it were of good things to come) to ye substance, & y^t wch seemed glorious hath no glory in respect of y^t wch excelleth; & all the sufferings y^t we have endured (from yo^u) for Christ hath not at all marrd his visage to us, but we still se more beauty in him; well knowing, y^t as they did unto him so they will doe unto us, & now they are come to pas, we remember y^t he said these things.

MARY TRASKE
MARGARET SMITH

From yor house of Correction where we have been unjustly restrained from o^r children & habitations one of us above tenn months & ye other about eight; & where we are yet continued by yor opressors y^t knows no shame;
Boston 21th of ye 10^mth 1660;

JOHN BURSTOW'S LETTER.[1]

The day of yu^r visitation is gon over yu^r heads: when yee had y^u light yee walked not in it; then darkness overtooke you & ye light judged & condemned you: then yee hated ye light because yu^r deeds wear evil, & now yee are in ye night wherin noe man can worke or doe any thing wch is exsepted of ye Lord. Your prayers are sinne & stinke, & an ill saver are you to ye Lord ou^r God, & yu^r assemblies are an abomination to ye Lord; yu^r hands are defiled wth blood: yu^r eyes are full of adultery & yu^r harts is as a caige of unclean spirits, & y^t wch should be a house of

---

[1] Massachusetts Archives, vol. x. p. 269.

APPENDIX.

prayer is become a denn of theives & robers, and yee comitt ludeness & are joyned wth ye destruction wch is swiftly coming upon you: yee y^t have an eare to heer, harken & com forth from among them, y^t yee may be as fier brands plucted out of ye fier, for as sartainely as ye plauges was powered forth upon hard harted Faro, shall ye plauges & judgements of ye Lord be powered forth upon ye inhabitanc of this towne of boston; & then yee shall know who are ye faulce prophets; wheather we wch pronounce judgements & plauges, or yu^r hierling prists wch spacke peace to you whilest you put into their mouth. And they are blind leaders of ye blind, & yee shall fall & perish: boath yee & yu^r prists whose king is the angell of ye botomless pit; & out of ye botomless pitt have thay their wisdom wch thay feede you wth; all wch is earthly, sencuall, divilish. And this earthly & durty wisdom is ye sarpents meat wch is had in you: but now is ye seed of ye woman made manifest to bruse ye sarpents head: and wee tread upon scorpions & handell sarpents & cast out unclean spirits by ye power of ye Lord, and thay cannot hurte or destroy, in all his holy mountaine.

Who can make a seperation betwixt ye preshous & ye ville amongst you: or who can deserne betwixt ye clean & ye unclean amongst you, for ye word of ye Lord is gon forth & ye decree of ye Lord is sealed, & thus it is fellen out to this wicked & untoward generation whose last estate is worse then their beginning; whose house was once swept and garnished, but a spirit seven times worse is entered into them & ye parfection of wickedness is among them. This is ye word of truth seen & declered in ye light wch tryeth and deserneth all spirits, wheather thay will heer or forbear. Saith ye Lord spacke thou unto them, but thay will not harken unto thee, for thay will not harken unto me, ye light wch reproveth them and woundeth them in ye secrets of their harts, but thay have revolted more & mor & have not greived nor remembred the affection of Joseph but have comitted whordoms against ye Lord and joyned wth ye adulterated spirit wch huntes after ye preshaus life to destroy it. There for y^t wch is for destruction to destruction, y^t wch is ye sword to ye sword, y^t wch is for fier to ye fier. And this shall be the end of them all: he y^t is unjust lett him be unjust still: he y^t is filthy lett him be filthy still, & he y^t is righteous let him be righteous still, & he y^t is holy let him be holy still. And to y^t wch yee are joyned to shall yee take yor portion. And ye reward of yu^r workes mine eye shall not pitty: or regard yu^r crye when in ye bitterness of yu^r soules yee cry out for ye extreame anguish & horror wch shall be on yu^r spirits; but as I have called & you regarded not, soe shall you call & cry, but I will not answer you wth ye least drope of water or mixtuer of peace to Ease y^t spirit, wch shall be tormented, but ye druges & ye cup shall yee drinke, wch is prepared for you wthout mixtuer. Lett not yu^r prists deceive you by spaking peace to you, for you & thay shall be cast into ye bed of torment together.

This is ye word of truth to you: Declared in ye Life & power of ye Lord.

JOHN. BURSTOW

Boston Jayell:
  The First day of ye 4 month
    1661.

LETTER FROM JOSIAH SUTHICK, A QUAKER, TO THE DEPUTIES ASSEMBLED IN THE GENERAL COURT.[1]

Freinds a few lines I thought good to lay before you, being moved by ye Lord therunto. . . . O freinds, for so I can call you: I am at enmiti with nothing in you but y^t wch sets it selfe ags^t ye libertie of ye Lords redeemed ones: wch is to serve ye Lord wth ye whole hart & ye spiret, & not in ye leter: whose praise is not of men but of God: what shall I say or how shall I speake unto you: let prejudices & ungrounded jelosies be set aside: and let us reason togeather: . . . take heed you take not ye place of God upon you to judg where God would hav you judg your selvs: for this know y^t ye god of heaven, hath searched our harts: & discovered to us ye truth, & for folowing & obeying ye truthe are wee made ofenders and transgressors of your lawes & hath rather chose to suffer under y^m nor obey y^m: because we have sertinly found y^t your wills & requireings have bene contrari unto ye will of our God,

[1] Massachusetts Archives, vol. x. pp. 251, 252.

therfore we dare not submit to y^m in obeying y^m: ... Did Christ persecute them y^t called him a blasphemer or did he desire ani bodili punishment on them y^t sayd hee cast out divells by belsebub ye princ of divells: is not his counsell other weise; did not he say love your enemies, bless y^m y^t curss you, doe good to y^m y^t hate you, pray for y^m y^t despitefully use you and persecute you: y^t yee may bee ye children of your father which is in heaven; for he maketh his sun to rise on ye just & on ye unjust: and maketh his rayne to rain on ye evile & on ye good: some have sayd wee were ye persecuters; but wee know wee are ye persecuted, yet wee can freely say, ye Lord lay not your sin to your charge, for I beleve mani of you know not what you doe: ... doth not Christ say, hee y^t smiteth thee on ye one cheek turn to him ye other also: have you such a spiret in you: ... is it y^t spiret y^t doth so rage when it is not honored or bowed too: consider your selvs & deale playnely wth your own harts be not deceivde ... have you not a law made by wch you can make all doe as you doe & as it were say as you say, or else to ye prisson & whiping poste: .... are you not out of ye right way: doe such actions proseed from the spirete of Christ or ye spiret of meeknes wch ye falen brother is to be recovered with: ... where Christ sayth doe good, there you doe evil: where hee sayth love, there do you hate: where hee sayth hold your hand, there doe you smite: where hee sayth judg your selvs, theire doe yee judg others & leave your selvs unjudged, & with y^t spiret wch is unjudged in your selvs, doe yee judg us & condemn us, but it revileth us not, for wee have y^t peec you cannot give nor take away: . . . But hee y^t knoweth my hart knoweth I desire nothing more then y^t you may know him & return unto him you have fought against: for what you doe unto any of Christ's servants, hee looks upon it as don unto himself: let these lines not be slited by you, but what you aprehend is not acording to truthe in y^m, let me have a reply derected unto a freind of ye Lord & a prissoner for keeping his commands : who am with held from my fameli vocations & kept in ye house of opression in boston. Known by name Josiah Suthick . . . From my hart I wish you may doe ye thing y^t is right before ye Lord: wch you will doe as his counsell you take : wch in a word is this; doe unto all men as yee would hav y^m doe unto you : & in y^t you will have peace : & wether you heare or forbeare, I am cleer of you before the Lord, the God of my salvation in whom I trust & desire for ever to follow & obey both in prosperiti and in adversity. J. S.

They lust after bloud, it is just with God they should have bloud to drink. From ye house of corection in boston, ye 21 of ye 8 moth 61.

For ye hands of ye Deputies in Generall, at present asembled in Boston. Let this be read amongst you, because it conserns you all.

INDEX.

ALLEN'S (R. H.) *New England Tragedies in Prose* criticised, 54, 73.
Ambrose, Alice, publicly whipped, 100.
Austin, Ann, arrives in Boston, 34; her arrest and persecution, 35-40.

Barclay, Robert, humiliates himself, 6-8; his views on the Scriptures, 18; on the civil law and magistracy, 26; his qualifications as a writer, 28.
Barclay's (Robert) *Apology*, 17, 28; *Catechism*, 28; *Anarchy of the Ranters*, 28.
Batter, Edmund, treasurer of Salem, 50; insults a Quaker woman, 51; attempts to sell the Southwicks, 52; persecutes the Quakers, 96.
Baxter, Richard, on the Inward Light, 19.
Bellingham, Gov. Richard, convenes the council for banishment of Ann Austin and Mary Fisher, 36; succeeds Endicott, 192; death of, 192.
Besse's (Joseph) *Collection of Sufferings*, 72, 183, 188.
Biddle, John, the father of English Unitarians, 4.
Bishop's (George) *New England Judged*, 30, 40, 43, 60, 70, 94, 96, 104, 162, 172, 175, 202.
"Body of the Liberties," the, extracts from, 34, 71.
Bowers, Barbara, trial of, 200.
Brend, William, barbarous treatment of, 57, 62-67.
Brewster, Margaret, 99, 104; trial of, 193-202.

Brigham, Judge William, on the Quakers in New Plymouth Colony, 115.
Brome's (James) *Travels over Scotland, England, and Wales*, 8, 10.
Bryant and Gay's *Popular History of the United States*, 105.
Burden, Anne, 111; imprisoned and banished, 112.
Burrough, Edward, 21, 25; his appeal to the King, 188.
Burstow, John, letter of, to his persecutors, 87, 217.

Carlyle's (Thomas) opinion of George Fox, 13.
Charles I., overthrow of, 2.
Charles II., King of England, orders laws against the Quakers suspended, 55, 189.
Chattam, Catherine, dresses in sackcloth and ashes, 97.
Chauncey, Charles, President of Harvard College, 94.
Christison, Wenlock, letter of, 60; sentenced to death, 61; his speech to the court, 87; harbored by Eliakim Wardwell, 100.
Coddington, William, 33.
Coercion and persecution under Charles II. and James II., 3.
Coit's (Thomas Winthrop) *Puritanism*, 10, 11, 12.
Coleman, Ann, torture of, 62, 99.
Colonial laws for suppression of the Quakers, 133-152.
Copeland, John, 111; petitions the King in behalf of the Massachusetts Quakers, 183-187.
Cotton, Rev. Seaborn, a persecutor of the Quakers, 100.

INDEX.

Cromwell, Oliver, 3.
Cudworth, James, proscribed for entertaining Quakers, 113; letter of, 114, 162.

Dexter's (Rev. H. M.) *As to Roger Williams*, 61; its calumnies against the Quakers, 73–75.
Dyer, Mary, sentenced to death, 58; reprieved and subsequently executed, 60; her letter to the General Court, 89; her courageous bearing, 111; letter of, 206.

Early Quakers, doctrines of the, 16–31.
Edwards, Thomas, publishes the *Grangraena*, 5.
Edmundson's (William) *Journal*, 97.
Ellis, Rev. George E., his treatment of the Quakers considered, 78, 129; his inconsistencies, 79–82.
Ellis's (Rev. George E.) *Massachusetts and its Early History*, 32, 82, 98, 125.
Ellwood, Thomas, 21.
Endicott, John, Governor of Massachusetts Colony, 33; bullies and threatens the Quakers, 43; denounced by Mary Prince, 44; fines Upsall, 48; defends execution of the Quakers, 59; sentences Christison to death, 62; letter of Mary Trask and Margaret Smith to, 84; receives and obeys the King's Missive, 191; renews his persecutions, 191; death of, 192.
Examination of Quakers in Boston, 157–161.

Fanaticism in the seventeenth century, 6, 9.
Featley, Rev. Dr. Daniel, his tract on the Anabaptists, 11; his hostility to Milton, 11.
Felton, Benjamin, 96.
Fisher, Mary, arrives in Boston, 34; her arrest and persecution, 35–40.
Fourbish, William, put in the stocks, 100.
Fiske's (John) careless repetition of slanders against the Quakers, 75–77.

Forster's (John) *Statesmen of England*, 9.
Fox, George, visits and speaks in steeple-houses, 5; the founder of Quakerism, 13; opinions of Macaulay and Carlyle concerning, 13; his parents, 14; early religious experience, 14; his mission revealed to him, 15; his views on magistracy, 25.

Gardner's (George) wife fined for absence from church, 128.
Gardner, Hored, whipping of, 116, 172.
Gibbons, Sarah, 96, 111, 116.
Gough's (John) *History of the Quakers*, 173.
Gould, Daniel, letter of, to the rulers and people of Boston, 90, 210.
Grahame's (James) *History of the Rise and Progress of the United States of North America*, 72.
Gunning, Dr., Bishop of Ely, 4.

Higginson, Rev. John, of Salem, 94, 95.
Hireling ministry, a, Milton's views concerning, 20.
Holder, Christopher, 111.
Hooten, Elizabeth, 94; barbarously whipped, 97; the first convert to Quakerism, 97; her sufferings, 177.
Hubberthorn, Richard, 26.
Hutchinson, Mrs. Ann, banished, 33.
Hutchinson Papers, the, 33, 94.

Inward Light, the, doctrine of, 16, 118, 132.
Ivimey's (Joseph) *Life and Times of John Milton*, 11, 12.

Janney's (Samuel M.) *Life of George Fox*, 29.
Jones, Margaret, 39; hanged for witchcraft, 41.

"King's Missive," the, 55, 189–191.
Kitchin, Elizabeth, insulted by Edmund Batter, 51.

Laud's (Archbishop) abortive at-

INDEX.   225

tempt to reconcile Rome and the Anglican Church, 2; execution of, 2.
Leddra, William, imprisoned and scourged, 62-64; put to death, 61; letter of, 208.
Lodge's (H. C.) *A Short History of the English Colonies in America*, 78.

Macaulay's (T. B.) estimate of George Fox, 13.
Marsden's (J. B.) *Later Puritans*, 10.
Massachusetts Archives, the, extracts from, 153-161, 182, 210, 213, 217, 220.
Massachusetts Historical Society, Proceedings of the, 82.
Massachusetts, General Court of, enacts laws against the Quakers, 45, 48, 49, 53; suspends and reënacts them, 55; employs John Norton to write a refutation of Quaker errors, 120; petitions to, against the Quakers, 121, 153.
Massachusetts Records, 70, 192; extracts from, 133-152, 175-177.
Masson's (David) *Life of Milton*, 5, 23.
Mather, Cotton, his abuse of the Quakers, 74; his *Magnalia*, 75.
Memorial History of Boston, the, 82, 85, 98, 111, 125.
Miles, Mary, trial of, 199.
Milton, John, epigram on the Presbyterians, 3; denounced as a pestilent Anabaptist, 11; anathematizes the Bishops, 11; replies to Salmasius's vindication of Charles I., 12; his views on a hireling ministry, 20.
"Minutes of the Magistrates" of Boston, 122.
Mott, Lucretia, 129.
Muggleton, Ludowick, 13.
Munster iniquities, the, 45, 46.

Naylor's (James) fantastic extravagances, 29.
Neal's (Daniel) *History of the Puritans*, 2, 8.
Newhouse, Thomas, 96, 104.
Newland, W., imprisoned, 114.
Norton, Humphrey, branded for heresy, 56; journal of, 92.

Norton, Rev. John, leading minister of the Massachusetts Colony, 33; his hatred of the Quakers, 57, 58, 67; his scriptural argument against them, 93, 120; recompensed therefor, 121; his defense of Brend's gaoler, 121.

Parker's (Hon. Joel) attack upon early Friends, 74.
Penn's (William) *Rise and Progress of the People called Quakers*, 29.
Petition, for severer laws against the Quakers, 121, 153; to the King for interference, 183-187.
Phelps, Nicholas, fined and imprisoned, 127.
Philanthrophy of the Quakers, 31.
Presbyterians, the, bigotry and cruelty of, 2; Milton's epigram on, 3.
Prince, Mary, denounces Endicott, 44; imprisonment of, 111.
Prynne's ridicule of church choirs, 11.
Puritanism, defined, 1; its growth and spread, 2-12; Quakerism an outgrowth of, 123.
Puritans, the English, Scriptural names adopted by, 8, 9; despoil churches and cathedrals, 10.
Puritans in Massachusetts, their persecutions of the Quakers, 32-68, 99-104, 126-128; their assertion that Quakers had no right to enter the colony refuted, 69-71; their strong and abusive language, 94; modern apologies for, 105; their accusations against the Quakers, 108; their abhorence of Quaker opinions the cause of the persecution, 117; their denunciations of the Inward Light, 118; their intolerance, 119; their plan of government a failure, 131.

"Quaker," a term applied in derision, 30.
Quakerism an outgrowth of Puritanism, 123.
Quakers, the, their doctrines and beliefs, 16-31; their views on the Inward Light, 16, 118; on

15

INDEX

liberty of thought and speech, 16 ; on the Scriptures, 17 ; on an ordained ministry and church tithes, 19, 20 ; on baptism, communion, prayers, and oaths, 22 ; on the Sabbath, 22 ; on titles, 22 ; on war, 23 ; on marriage, 23 ; a law-abiding people, 25 ; persecution of, 29 ; style themselves Friends, 30 ; their test of membership, 30 ; modes of procedure, 30, 31 ; philanthropy, 31 ; arrival of Quaker missionaries at Boston, Massachusetts, 32, 34 ; their arrest, 35 ; abuse and banishment of, 38-40 ; arrival of others at Boston, 42 ; more imprisoned and banished, 42 ; the General Court enacts laws against, 45, 48, 49, 53 ; women stripped and whipped, 51, 62 ; falsely branded as vagabonds, 53 ; temporarily relieved by the "King's Missive," 55 ; mutilated, hanged, banished, and scourged, 56, 57, 62-66 ; popular sympathy with, 57-59, 66-68 ; their right to enter the colony, 69, 70 ; four fifths of them residents before the persecution, 71 ; slanders against, 72-74 ; their treatment by modern "historians," 75-82 ; their testimonies considered and vindicated, 82-91 ; not guilty as a body, of improper behavior, 91 ; special accusations against examined, 94 ; the cases of Lydia Wardwell and Deborah Wilson, 99-104 ; interruptions of church service, 107 ; their custom of wearing the hat, 109 ; persecution of, in the Plymouth Colony, 114 ; their religious opinions the real cause of the persecution, 117 ; their leading tenets common with those of the Puritans, 117 ; radical differences,119; summary of prosecutions against, in Boston, 122 ; themselves Puritans, 125 ; their final triumph, 128 ; their religion still an active force, 132 ; colonial laws for their suppression, 133-152 ; examination of, in Boston, 157-161 ;

order of banishment, 182 ; petition the King to interfere, 183 ; the King's Missive, 189, 190 ; proscriptive laws reënacted, 191 ; trials of, 193-202 ; letters of William Robinson, Marmaduke Stevenson, Mary Dyer, and other leading Friends, 202-222.

Rayner, Rev., instigates whipping of Quaker women, 100.
Religious controversy and debate in England during the seventeenth century, 3.
Robinson, William, sentenced to death, 58 ; letter of, 202.
Roots, Thomas, 96.
Rouse, John, petitions the King in behalf of the Massachusetts Quakers, 183-187.

Saltonstall, Sir Richard, deplores persecution of the Quakers, 33.
Scriptures, the, Quaker views concerning, 17.
Scudder, H. E., 124.
Sects in the seventeenth century enumerated, 5.
Sewall's (Judge Samuel) definition of Quakerism, 75 ; *Diary*, 99.
Sewel's (William) *History of the Quakers*, 23, 29, 177, 188, 206, 208.
Shattuck, Samuel, petitions the King in behalf of the Massachusetts Quakers, 183.
Skerry, Henry, 96.
Smith, Margaret, letter of, to Governor Endicott, 84, 213.
Smith, Richard, 111.
Southcote, Joanna, 13.
Southwick, Consader, 122.
Southwick, Daniel and Provided, ordered to be sold into slavery, 50 ; Provided fined, 127.
Southwick, Josiah, addresses a letter to the General Court, 88, 175, 220.
Southwick (Southick), Laurence and Cassandra, sufferings of, 173 ; Laurence, letter of, 175.
Stevenson, Marmaduke, sentenced to death, 58 ; letter of, 202.

INDEX.

Temple, Col., endeavors to prevent execution of Quakers, 60.
Thirstone, Thomas, 111.
Toleration fostered under the Commonwealth, 3.
Tomkins, Mary, publicly whipped, 100.
Trask, Mary, letter of, to Governor Endicott, 84, 213.

Upsall, Nicholas, sends provisions to imprisoned Quakers, 36; laments anti-Quaker legislation, 47; fined and banished, 48.

Vane, Sir Henry, 3, 33.
Very, Nathaniel, 129.

Wardwell, Eliakim, 99; put in the stocks, 100.
Wardwell, Lydia, case of, 102; her cruel punishment, 104.

Wardwell, Thomas, 99.
Waugh, Dorothy, 96, 111, 116.
Whitehead, Mary, 111.
Whiting, John, refutes Cotton Mather's slanders, 76.
Whiting's (John) *Truth and Innocency Defended*, 74, 76.
Whittier's (John G.) lines on Cassandra Southwick, 53; poem on the King's Missive, 189.
Williams, Roger, driven into exile, 33.
Wilson, Deborah, the case of, 104.
Winthrop, John, Governor of Connecticut, protests against hanging Quakers, 60.
Winthrop, John, Governor of Massachusetts, regrets his persecution of "heresy," 33.
Winthorp, Samuel, son of Gov. Winthrop, a Quaker, 71.
Wright, Lydia, trial of, 197.